PLATO'S 'EUTHYPHRO' AND THE EARLIER THEORY OF FORMS

International Library of Philosophy and Scientific Method

EDITOR: TED HONDERICH

A Catalogue of books already published in the
International Library of Philosophy and Scientific Method
will be found at the end of this volume.

Plato's 'Euthyphro'
and the
Earlier Theory
of Forms

by

R. E. Allen

NEW YORK
HUMANITIES PRESS

First published
in the United States of America 1970
by Humanities Press Inc.
303 Park Avenue South
New York, N.Y. 10010
© *R. E. Allen 1970*
SBN 391 00055 1

Printed in Great Britain

CONTENTS

To

LEVI ARNOLD POST

Professor of Greek Emeritus
in
Haverford College

Et melior doctrina imbutus

PREFACE

Between 1880 and 1924 there were seven editions of the *Euthyphro* published in English alone; since 1924 there have been none. Fashions change in scholarship, as in clothes.

Yet the *Euthyphro* is worth studying. It gives as clear a picture as we have of Socratic dialectic in operation, and of the connection of that dialectic with Plato's earlier theory of Forms. It also gives a clear picture of one (*one*) aspect of Greek religion. If these are primarily historical considerations, there is a reason for studying the dialogue which is merely human. The *Euthyphro* is the portrait of an extraordinary mind at work on issues which, though now differently phrased, have not become irrelevant.

This version of the dialogue is a translation with interspersed comment. The comment does not pretend to the status of a commentary; it is meant partly as a help to the Greekless reader in finding his way, and partly as a means of embedding the discussion of the earlier theory of Forms which follows it.

The argument of the second and longer part of this book is that there *is* an earlier theory of Forms, found in the *Euthyphro* and other early dialogues as an essential adjunct of Socratic dialect: the widely held opinion that there is no such theory rests on a variety of misunderstandings and distortions of Plato's text. The theory of Forms in the early dialogues, however, is not the theory of Forms found in middle dialogues such as the *Phaedo* and *Republic*: they differ on the crucial issue of ontological status.

I have not offered a text, believing that the labour of the undertaking would have been out of proportion to its usefulness.

My obligations are various. To Harold Cherniss I owe a debt of friendship and instruction which in the nature of the case I cannot easily repay. I have consulted John Burnet's and W. A. Heidel's editions of the *Euthyphro* often, especially in making the translation, and always with profit; my debt to them is too frequent always to be indicated, but those who know their work will know it is there. I have also to thank Gregory Vlastos and David Furley, both for personal kindnesses and for instruction which saved errors. Gates Agnew, William Eddy, and F. W. Householder have offered generous criticism. The Bollingen Foundation provided me with leisure, and the Institute for Advanced Study ideal conditions for work. As always, my greatest debt is to Ann Usilton Allen, my wife.

PRINCETON, NEW JERSEY.

BIBLIOGRAPHICAL ABBREVIATIONS

Euthyphro John Burnet, *Plato's Euthyphro, Apology and Crito*, Oxford, 1924.

ACPA H. F. Cherniss, *Aristotle's Criticism of Plato and the Academy*, vol. i, Baltimore, 1944.

DK H. Diels, and W. Kranz, *Die Fragmente der Vorsokratiker* (8th ed.), Berlin, 1956.

LSJ Liddell and Scott, Jones, *A Greek-English Lexicon* (9th ed.), Oxford, 1951.

PC F. M. Cornford, *Plato's Cosmology*, London, 1937.

PED R. Robinson, *Plato's Earlier Dialectic* (2nd ed.), Oxford, 1948.

PP F. M. Cornford, *Plato and Parmenides*, London, 1939.

PTI W. D. Ross, *Plato's Theory of Ideas*, Oxford, 1951.

PTK F. M. Cornford, *Plato's Theory of Knowledge*, London, 1935.

REA H. F. Cherniss, *The Riddle of the Early Academy*, Berkeley and Los Angeles, 1945.

SPM R. E. Allen (ed.), *Studies in Plato's Metaphysics*, London, 1965.

I

INTRODUCTION

I. THE PLACE OF THE *Euthyphro* IN PLATO'S DIALOGUES

The *Euthyphro* is an early dialogue, written after the death of Socrates in 399 B.C., and before Plato's first visit to Italy and Sicily in 388–7. It ranks, then, with the *Apology, Crito, Laches, Lysis, Charmides, Hippias Major* and *Minor, Ion, Euthydemus,* and *Protagoras,* other works of Plato's early period.[1]

It is difficult to assign even a probable order of composition to these dialogues: considerations of style and language will not serve, and there is little else in the way of direct evidence. But the *Protagoras,* which is by far the longest and most artistically complex, should be put late in the period, and the *Euthydemus,* by reason of content and similar structure, probably belongs with it; both dialogues are narrated, with dramatic introductions – an experiment Plato was to repeat again, flawlessly, in the *Phaedo.* The *Euthyphro,* by contrast, is cast in simple dramatic form throughout, and for that reason, and perhaps also because it was placed first in the first tetralogy by Thrasyllus, who edited Plato's works in the reign of Tiberius, it has come to be regarded as one of the earliest dialogues Plato wrote, and perhaps even the first. But the Thrasyllean arrangement is not based on order of composition,[2] and if complexity argues lateness, it hardly follows that

---

[1] This list is conjectural, and its order for the most part arbitrary. For a summary of other conjectures, by no means exhaustive, see *PTI,* ch. i.

The inclusion of the *Hippias Major* here is open to particular question. I shall treat it as authentic and early, but it has been suspect on both counts, and no point in the argument will be allowed to turn on its unsupported evidence.

[2] As Burnet remarked, '(The *Euthyphro's*) position as the first dialogue of the first tetralogy is due solely to the consideration that, in the story of the trial and death of Socrates, it comes before the *Apology,* just as the *Crito* comes after it' (*Euthyphro,* p. 4).

what is simple is therefore early. It is enough to know that the *Euthyphro* was probably written in the first decade of the fourth century, when Plato was in his thirties. Whatever its exact date, he was already master of his craft.

2. THE TEXT

The text of the *Euthyphro* here used is Burnet's. I have departed from it at 14c, 3–4, where conflict in the manuscript tradition indicates antique corruption, and Burnet's editorial conservatism has produced, in this case, a poor sense. The reading here adopted is Schanz's; it is supported by Ficino,[1] and by Burnet's *versio Armeniaca*. I have also accepted, on grounds of sense, a conjecture of Heidel's in 8d, 10.

The present state of Plato's text, at least for the first seven tetralogies, has been described by Professor Dodds as follows:[2]

> To this day no one can say with certainty how many primary witnesses to the text there are, or how they are related to each other and to the secondary MSS. The main cause of this ignorance is the lack of trustworthy collations. There are at least 64 extant MSS. which contain the *Gorgias* or part of it. Of these only two, B and T, have been accurately collated in their entirety. In *Gorgias*, a third primary witness, W, has hitherto been known only from a few selected readings; a fourth, F, has been gravely misreported. For most of the remaining MSS. we are still dependent on the notoriously unreliable collations of Bekker and Stallbaum; some have never been collated at all.

An unfortunate situation, which Professor Dodd's own edition of the *Gorgias*, and the late R. S. Bluck's of the *Meno*, have done much to correct. But it does not follow from the fact that the evidential basis for Plato's text is incompletely established, and sometimes falsely reported, that the text itself is in any radical way unsound. It is in fact one of the least corrupt of any which have come down from classical antiquity, and future editions, though they will improve its *apparatus criticus*, are unlikely to much alter

---

[1] Perhaps evidence, which R. S. Bluck (*Plato's* Meno, p. 145) failed to find for the *Meno,* that Ficino had access to sources independent of the traditions represented by BTWPF.

[2] E. R. Dodds, *Plato's* Gorgias, p. 34.

understanding of its sense.[1] There are, at least, no issues of importance to the interpretation of the *Euthyphro* which hinge on a question of text.

3. TRANSLATION

I have attempted to render the *Euthyphro* simply, in English of no particular date or place, and in rhythms approximating those of speech. The translation is not meant to be colloquial. Those who believe that when Euthyphro says πάνυ γε he means 'Uh huh,' or that κινδυνεύει may on occasion be rendered 'Um . . . ah . . . yes,' may hie themselves to Professor Richards,[2] where they will find an overset more in the swing of things.

To translate is to interpret, well or ill. There is really no such thing as literalness. But where Plato's language bears on the reader's understanding of the theory of Forms, I have attempted to let the Greek show itself through the English, and bring the meaning out of the text as directly and neutrally as possible. Thus, for example, adjectival abstracts may be formed in Greek as we form them in English, by adding a suffix which does the work of '-ness' to the adjective stem; or they may be formed by the neuter singular adjective and its agreeing article; or even, sometimes, by the neuter singular adjective alone. I have undertaken to render the Greek with an English expression formed in a parallel way, by, for example, 'holiness', 'the holy' or 'holy', as the case requires.

This does not make for idiomatic English. It is rather an example of that mixture of English vocabulary and Greek syntax which produces the various dialects of Translatorese. But it is not meaningless, as has sometimes been maintained, and there is a reason for it. Unless it is done, much of the difficulty Euthyphro has in satisfying Socrates' demand to know what the holy is will seem quite unintelligible. Expressions such as ὅσιον and

---

[1] Thus, for example, Bluck's text of the *Meno* differs from Burnet's in something over thirty readings. Only a few of these were prompted by fresh evidence, as distinct from editorial opinion, and none produces a change in sense likely to affect interpretation. Dodds, in the Preface to his edition of the *Gorgias,* remarks: 'I am conscious that very few of the textual problems I have discussed affect our understanding of Plato's thought.'

[2] I. A. Richards, *Why So, Socrates?*

τὸ ὅσιον have a range of meaning, and a pattern of emphasis within that range, which corresponding abstract nouns in English lack; but the use of these expressions is not so remote that it cannot be caught, and at the risk of some clumsiness it has seemed best to try to catch it. If the reader finds talk of 'holy' or 'the holy' sometimes puzzling, he may reflect that Euthyphro finds it sometimes puzzling too.

There is a further point. Euthyphro and Socrates are 2,500 years distant from us in time, and their patterns of thought are different from our own. It is no disservice to them or to ourselves if they are made to speak in such a way as to recall that fact. It is not wrong to give their speech the accent of remoteness. It has been said that the right aim of translation is to produce that effect upon the reader which the author intended for the original. In the case of ancient authors, this is one ideal which is often a good deal the worse for being unrealizable; ancient authors did not write for modern readers, but for men of their own time, and a smooth modern version will often distort by making familiar what is in fact strange.

The passage of time has given Plato's dialogues, and especially the early ones, a quality they did not originally have: they have come to be parts of that peculiar species of poetry which the late G. M. Trevelyan called the poetry of history:[1]

> The poetry of history lies in the quasi-miraculous fact that once, on this earth, once, on this familiar spot of ground, walked other men and women, as actual as we are today, thinking their own thoughts, swayed by their own passions, but now all gone, one generation vanishing after another, gone as utterly as we ourselves shall shortly be gone like ghost at cock-crow. This is the most familiar and certain fact about life, but it is also the most poetical, and the knowledge of it has never ceased to entrance me, and to throw a halo of poetry round the dustiest record that Dryasdust can bring to light.

Trevelyan found in the offerings of Dryasdust a thing Keats found in a Grecian urn, and a thing many readers of Plato – especially those whose sensibilities have not been hardened by professional study – find in the early dialogues. The *Euthyphro* is a work of philosophy; but it is also a foster-child of Silence and slow Time, and in the translation which follows I have tried, with

[1] G. M. Trevelyan, *An Autobiography*, p. 13.

4

what success I cannot say, to preserve something of the poetry of its pastness.

4. DRAMATIC STRUCTURE

The structure of the *Euthyphro* is serial. After a lengthy introduction – lengthy in relation to the total bulk of the dialogue – Socrates introduces the question, 'What is the holy?' When the ground has been cleared of the attempt to answer that question by naming examples, Euthyphro offers four definitions: that the holy is what is loved by the gods; that it is what is loved by all the gods; that it is service to the gods; and that it is an art of prayer and sacrifice. The second and fourth definitions are dialectically derivative, respectively, from the first and third, to which they are conjoined. There is an interlude between the second and third definitions, followed by a discussion of what proper definition requires. There is a further break between the first and second definitions, which I have called an interlude, but which also serves to advance discussion.

It may be asked what bearing, if any, this structure has on the interpretation of the dialogue. Julius Stenzel held that,[1]

> It suits Plato's temperament to insinuate part of his meaning by artistic, or formal, devices. His whole meaning is not always conveyed in plain words, as it is with a thinker who regards expression as a secondary matter.

This is surely sometimes true, and the interpretation of dialogues such as the *Parmenides* and *Sophist*, or, for that matter, the *Meno* and *Protagoras*, has suffered for ignoring it. But if it is sometimes true, it is not always true. It goes without saying that literary analysis may be relevant to the interpretation of any of the dialogues. But that literary analysis will prove to have philosophical implications is a matter to be settled on the merits of individual cases, which is to say, on the basis of evidence. *Formgeschichte* is not a universal panacea, and it cannot be mechanically applied. So far as the *Euthyphro* is concerned, its relevance is slight: no substantive issue in the interpretation of the dialogue turns on it.

---

[1] As summarized by D. J. Allan, *Plato's Method of Dialectic,* p. viii.

5. INTERPRETATION

The interpretation of the *Euthyphro* offered here is analytic, in this precise sense, that it is an analysis of the dialogue and its arguments. Of interpretation in the grander sense there is none. George Grote, over one hundred years ago, gave what I take to be a true view of the dialogue:[1]

> Euthyphro is a man who feels unshaken confidence in his own knowledge, and still more in his own correct religious belief. Socrates appears in his received character as confessing ignorance, soliciting instruction, and exposing inconsistencies and contradiction in what is given him for instruction. We must . . . take this ignorance on the part of the Platonic Socrates not as assumed, but as very real. In no part of the Platonic writings do we find any tenable definition of the Holy and the Unholy, such as is here demanded of Euthyphro. The Talent of Socrates consists in exposing bad definitions, not in providing good ones.

The search for definition in the *Euthyphro* ends in failure. The dialogue does not say what holiness is, or what religion ought to be, and if Plato had views on either of these subjects, he has not here told us what they are. There has been no drought of critics willing to make good the omission for him; but their speculations testify mainly to the inveterate scholarly habit of finding doctrine where Plato offered dialectic. The *Euthyphro*, if it suggests much, concludes little. It is an exercise in dialectic, and it is as dialectic that it must be understood.

One persistent misinterpretation of the dialogue has arisen out of 13e, where it is suggested that holiness may be service of men to gods in producing noble products. This definition is rejected, because it turns out to be impossible to say what those products are.[2] But Adam urged this as a reason for accepting the definition, supporting his contention with 'Bonitz's Principle' that, 'Whatever remains unrefuted in a Platonic dialogue contains the key to its positive teaching.'[3] This principle, a false generalization of *Gorgias*, 527b, is itself here misapplied: the claim that there are noble products which the gods produce with the help of men is not refuted because it is never made. Only the possibility is entertained.

---

[1] *Plato and Other Companions of Socrates* vol. i, pp. 322–3.
[2] See below, pp. 57–58, and Burnet, *Euthyphro*, p. 57.
[3] J. Adam, *Plato's* Euthyphro, p. xii.

Burnet, having seen that the dialogue is not meant to affirm that holiness is service of men to gods in producing noble products, supposed that the dialogue is meant to deny it:[1]

> If there were any definite ἔργον which the gods produce with our help, it must indeed be something 'mighty fine'. But in fact there is none, since ὁσιότης is no specialized art but a condition of the soul (ἕξις ψυχῆς). That is the positive result which the *Euthyphro* is meant to suggest to those who know the true Socratic doctrine, though it is nowhere explicitly stated.

But surely, if the *Euthyphro* were meant to suggest that holiness is not an art with a product, but a condition of soul, it would have suggested it. In fact, neither Adam nor Burnet are right, for the dialogue takes no stand on the issue over which they disagree. It is, perhaps one virtue of attending to dialectic rather than doctrine that one need not invent what one does not find.

There is a second persistent misinterpretation of the *Euthyphro*, arising from a connection conjectured for it with other dialogues. The misinterpretation may be one of great antiquity. Diogenes Laertius (III, 62) reports the existence of an edition of Plato by Aristophanes of Byzantium, in the late second century B.C. That edition was arranged in trilogies, perhaps on the analogy of Attic drama, and one of those trilogies consisted of the *Euthyphro, Apology,* and *Theaetetus.* What prompted this connection? Possibly only the chronological details of scene-setting. But possibly also this: the *Apology* portrays Socrates as undertaking his moral mission to the Athenians at the behest of the god at Delphi; the *Theaetetus* claims that the moral aim for men is to 'become like god as far as possible', which means becoming 'just and holy with wisdom' (176a–b); and the *Euthyphro* attempts to define holiness. All this is heady stuff. Combine it with the fact that the *Theaetetus* closes with Socrates on his way to the Porch of the King Archon to answer the indictment of Meletus, and that it is at that Porch on that occasion where the scene of the *Euthyphro* is placed, and it is the stuff of which interpretations are made. The changes are easily rung. Holiness implies the imitation of god; the imitation of god implies wisdom; wisdom implies philosophy; philosophy implies the contemplation of true being; the *Euthyphro* undertakes to define holiness;

---

[1] *Euthyphro*, p. 57.

therefore, the *Euthyphro* is meant to show that 'true' holiness is philosophy; or perhaps that 'true' religion implies the discovery of 'the metaphysical'.

Unfortunately, there is not a word in the *Euthyphro* to suggest that it is the moral duty of men to become like god, or gods. The *Euthyphro* cannot be interpreted through the *Theaetetus* in any case, since the *Theaetetus* was written after 369 B.C., and at least twenty years, or perhaps closer to thirty, separate it from the *Euthyphro*. If that consideration does not dampen the unquenchable enthusiasm of critics, it may be reflected that no reader, however ingenious, could draw such conclusions as these from the *Euthyphro* itself, a fact which may perhaps be thought sufficient reason to reject them as an interpretation of the *Euthyphro*. Once again, it is better to attend to dialectic rather than to doctrine, for attention to doctrine leads to invention.

There is a third common misinterpretation. It is often claimed that the purpose of the *Euthyphro* is apologetic in a way in which other early dialogues are not. Surely it is no accident, it is held, that Socrates should be made to discuss holiness or piety at a time when he has just been indicted for corrupting the youth and for impiety. Following up this clue, Adam thought that the figure of *Euthyphro* was meant to represent 'active and consistent' Athenian orthodoxy; that Socrates, by refuting Euthyphro's mistaken notions about holiness, is refuting the charge of impiety for which he was tried and condemned; and that the dialogue itself was meant to show the Athenians that their religion was 'virtually dead', so as to pave the way for a 'higher creed'.

This interpretation does not simply improve upon the text; it contradicts it. It is itself an interesting question what the word 'orthodox' means when applied to Athenian religion. But whatever it is taken to mean, its use can hardly be compatible with Euthyphro's moral and theological views (4d–5a), nor with the fact that he is frequently laughed to scorn in the Assembly (3c, 9b), presumably by the very men who convicted Socrates, nor with the fact that he has an extravagant admiration for Socrates and regards Meletus' prosecution as injuring the city at its very hearth (3a–b). But it is perhaps sufficient to reflect that, if you mean to attack 'orthodoxy' to any purpose, you do well not to choose an eccentric as its representative. If there is an apologetic message to the *Euthyphro*, it is the familiar Socratic message that before you indict a man for impiety, it is good to know what piety is.

There is room for an interpretation of the *Euthyphro* which will examine the structure of its arguments, the fit of their premisses and conclusions, their assumptions, and their sense. And there is a general consideration which may be urged in favour of such an undertaking. Socratic dialectic is an activity, not a body of propositions; it is therefore reasonable to suppose that to understand the *Euthyphro* is to understand the dialectical work which is being done in it, not some propositional product to which that work is only a means.

To say this is, of course, not to say that the *Euthyphro* has no determinate philosophical content. The dialectic of the dialogue is founded on assumptions about the essence or nature of things which regulate its work. If that work ends in failure, with no definition of holiness achieved, the touchstone of failure lies precisely in the rules which guided the search. Those rules imply assumptions in metaphysics. Specifically, I shall argue, they imply a theory of Forms.

6. THE *Euthyphro* AND GREEK RELIGION

The theme of the *Euthyphro*, or at least its theme in counterpoint, is religion. The modern reader will find little in its treatment which is familiar, and much that is strange. Religion to him is liable to mean personal religion, with its concern for the inner life of the worshipper, and the inward relation of the soul to God. The religion of the *Euthyphro* belongs to a different world of ideas – so different a world, in fact, that some readers may hesitate to call it religion at all.

That world is usually described as Homeric or Olympian, but this is so only under qualification. Euthyphro stands to Homer and Hesiod in much the way that a modern Fundamentalist stands to Holy Writ: his beliefs, extreme as they are, have their proof texts; but the texts, treated with great literalness, are selectively chosen.

The proof texts, certainly, may be turned up with ease. The Zeus of the *Iliad* is a tyrant of more than human power, and more than human failing. The lord of heaven and earth, he won his place by violence, and rules by force. There is a generosity of scale about him which is no doubt admirable; the mere catalogue of his philanderings (which, by a happy thought, it occurs to him to offer Hera, his wife) fills twelve dense lines of hexameter verse, and it is well known with what ingenuity he accomplished them. He was not all-powerful: he could not, for example, save Hector, who was dearest to him of all mortals, for Fate prevented. But he was more powerful than any other god, or all the gods together, a fact which was a source of pleasure to him:[1]

> Among the other gods fell grievous bitter strife, and their hearts were carried diverse in their breasts. And they clashed together with a great noise, and the wise earth groaned, and the clarion of great Heaven rang around. Zeus heard as he sat upon Olympus, and his heart within him laughed pleasantly when he beheld the strife of the gods.

In addition to his pleasant sense of humour, he had a short and nasty temper.

If you take all this literally, if you people your Olympus with a crew of squabbling deities, presided over by a High God who is dangerous as a volcano and unpredictable as lightning and something of a cad, it is liable to affect your religion. Such gods are forces which may perhaps be propitiated or enlisted in your service: you will expect to do business with them. But you are not likely to regard them as lords of a moral order, or recognize in or through them a binding claim on conduct. Lowes Dickenson summed up matters thus:[2]

> The gods of Greece were beings essentially like man, superior to him not in spiritual or even in moral attributes, but in outward gifts, such as strength, beauty, and immortality. And as a consequence of this his relations to them were not inward and spiritual, but external and mechanical. In the midst of a crowd of deities, capricious and conflicting in their wills, he had to find his way as best he could. There was no knowing what a god might want; there was no knowing what he might be going to do. If a man fell into trouble, no doubt he had offended somebody, but it was not easy to say whom or how; if he neglected the proper observances no doubt he would be punished, but it was not everyone who knew what the proper observances were. Altogether it was a difficult thing to ascertain or move the will of the gods, and one must help oneself as best one could. The Greek, accordingly,

[1] *Iliad,* xxi, 385 ff., trans. Lang, Leaf and Myers.
[2] *The Greek View of Life,* pp. 18–19.

helped himself by an elaborate system of sacrifice and prayer and divination, a system which had little connection with an internal and spiritual life, but the object of which was simply to discover and if possible to affect the divine purposes. This is what we meant by saying that the Greek view of the relation of man to the gods was mechanical.

This is an accepted portrait of Greek religion, and certainly it fits the *Euthyphro*. If religion proceeds on such assumptions as these, prayer and sacrifice will not involve, as the *Prayer Book* has it, 'the outward and visible sign of an inward and spiritual grace', a sacrament; they will rather involve, as Socrates points out at 14e, a business transaction. Religion becomes a contract, and hopefully a bargain (cf. 15a) – *do ut des*. Lowes Dickenson called the relation mechanical; it might also have been called magical. Olympian religion had chthonian roots.

But if there was this to it, this was not all there was to it. Homer's gods are perhaps all too human; but in them, or through them, it is possible to discern elements which go beyond mythology, and cross boundaries of language and custom and time. Professor Guthrie has said: 'The sway of Homer's literary creations over Greek religious thought was certainly artificial, and indeed a hindrance to the development of a real and inward religion.'[1] Perhaps this is true. But religion is a matter, not merely of myth, or creed and theology, but of art and ritual and the promptings of the heart; and if myths and creeds seem empty when viewed from without, they have a meaning and a numinous significance to those who use them quite beyond their manifest content.[2] Homer may have made things too precise, may have shaped and hardened outlines in such a way as to turn mystery into paradox for later generations. But those who find Greek religion spiritually sterile may consider a prayer of Electra, cited and translated by Professor Guthrie. It is offered before the altar of Apollo after eight years of captivity and insult:[3]

O Lord Apollo, graciously hear their prayer, and hear me also, who so oft have come before thine altar with such gifts as my devout hand could bring. And now, O Lycean Apollo, with all my strength I beseech thee – I fall before thee – I implore thee: be

[1] *The Greeks and Their Gods,* p. 276.
[2] Cf. E. R. Goodenough, *Jewish Symbols in the Greco-Roman Period,* vol. iv, pp. 28 ff.
[3] Sophocles, *Electra,* 1,376 ff.

thou provident in aiding these our counsels, and show unto men
the rewards of the wicked, how they are dealt with by the gods.

This is Sophocles, not Homer. But it shows matter in Olympian
religion with which the mind of a Sophocles might deal.

7. THE *Euthyphro* AND THE HISTORICAL SOCRATES

A word should perhaps be said, for tradition's sake, about the
so-called 'Socratic Problem', the problem of the relation of the
historical Socrates to the Socrates of the dialogues.

John Singleton Copley once remarked that a portrait was a
picture with 'a little something funny about the mouth'. It is not
the least virtue of Plato's portrait of Socrates in the early dialogues
that it is not only instinct with life, but conveys something of that
power of mind and personality which so indelibly marked the
generation of philosophers which followed, men as diverse in
outlook and temperament as Antisthenes, Aristippus, and Plato
himself.

In the middle dialogues, Plato's purpose was to present a
comprehensive vision of the world and man's place in it; and the
figure of Socrates there becomes a visible token of the music
which is philosophy, the contemplation of what always is and
never changes. But in the early dialogues, Plato's purpose was
different; importantly, it was to justify the life of Socrates and
describe his peculiar mission to Athens, and to defend his memory
against vilifications circulated after his death. But Socrates could
not have been defended by presenting to those who had known
him a picture which in any serious way was false. This is a reason
to suppose that the early dialogues provide, not only a portrait of
Socrates, but a good likeness.[1] It may be that there is an element –

---

[1] This has been doubted, because Plato's portrait differs from those drawn by
other contemporaries. The latter, however, suffer from obvious defects. Aristophanes drew Socrates in the *Clouds* as part Sophist and part natural philosopher; that
was burlesque. Xenophon drew him, in the *Memorabilia* and elsewhere, as a fifth-
century Samuel Johnson, a dealer in wise adages and sound common sense; he was
more, for otherwise he would not have been put to death by the Athenians, or
reverenced afterwards by Platonists, Stoics, Cynics, and Hedonists alike. Of
Aeschines of Sphettos, nothing now remains but a few fragments, conjecturally
restored (for which see G. C. Field, *Plato and His Contemporaries*, pp. 146–57, and
H. Dittmar, *Aischines von Sphettos*). Each of these men viewed Socrates from a
perspective whose co-ordinates were defined by their own peculiar intentions and,

a far smaller element than in the middle dialogues, surely – of idealization in the early dialogues: Plato, reflecting on the pattern of Socrates' peculiar questioning, may have been led to views about Forms and the world which Socrates himself never entertained. This question cannot now be answered; nor perhaps could Plato himself have answered it, have stated clearly the difference between what, as an artist, he had invented and what he had found. But truth has hardly suffered because the artist was a philosopher of genius.

---

perhaps even more importantly, their own peculiar understanding of the world. That type of perspective is not invariant under projection – not in the biography of any man, and certainly not in the biography of a man at once so simple and so complex as Socrates. Socrates is one of those few in the history of the world who have been condemned by their fellows as criminals, and afterwards worshipped by their fellows as saints. Such men are not easily understood at best. They are certainly not understood by men like Xenophon and Aristophanes, soldiers and comic poets.

II

THE *EUTHYPHRO*

We talked of translation. I said, I could not define it, nor could I think of a similitude to illustrate it; but that it appeared to me the translation of poetry could be only imitative. JOHNSON: You may translate books of science exactly. You may also translate history, in so far as it is not embellished with oratory, which is poetical. Poetry, indeed, cannot be translated; and therefore, it is the poets that preserve languages; for we would not be at the trouble to learn a language, if we could have all that is written in it just as well in a translation. But as the beauties of poetry cannot be preserved in any language except that in which it was originally written, we learn the language.

Boswell's *Life of Dr. Johnson*, LL.D.

I. CHARACTERS AND SETTING (2A–5C)

The scene is Athens, at the Porch of the King Archon. The year is 399 B.C. Socrates, now seventy years old, has come for a hearing on the charge of impiety brought against him by Meletus, a charge which will lead to his conviction and death. Euthyphro has come to prosecute his aged father for murder.

The King was the second of nine archons provided by the Athenian Constitution. He had oversight of religious observance and religious law, and specifically over legal cases involving impiety and homicide. An official chosen by lot, he was King by inheritance: in ancient times, the kings had represented and interceded for their people with the gods, a task the democratic magistrate continued to perform. 'To him who has obtained the office of King have been assigned the most solemn and peculiarly ancestral of the ancient observances.'[1]

---

[1] *Politicus*, 290e, trans. W. K. C. Guthrie. *Cf.* Aristotle, *Ath. Resp.*, 57.

Socrates   *Euthyphro*

2a   *E.* What happened, Socrates, to make you leave your
accustomed pastimes in the Lyceum and spend
your time here today at the King's Porch? You
can hardly have a suit pending before the King, as
I do.

     S. In Athens, Euthyphro, it is not called a suit, but an
indictment.

b   *E.* Really? Someone must have indicted you. For I will
not suspect you of indicting someone else.

     S. Certainly not.

     E. But someone has indicted you?

     S. Yes.

     E. Who is he?

     S. I do not know the man well, Euthyphro; it appears to
me that he is young and not prominent. His name,
I think, is Meletus. He belongs to the deme
of Pitthus, if you recall a Pitthean Meletus with
lanky hair and not much beard, but a hooked
nose.

c   *E.* I have not noticed him, Socrates. But what is the
charge?

     S. Charge? One that does him credit, I think. It is no small
thing, young as he is, to be knowledgeable in so
great a matter; for he says he knows how the youth
are being corrupted and who is corrupting them.
No doubt he is wise, and realizing that, in my
ignorance, I corrupt his comrades, he comes to the
city as to a mother to accuse me. He alone seems to
me to begin his political career correctly; for the

d   correct way to begin is to look after the young men
of the City first, so that they will be as good as
possible, just as a good farmer naturally looks after
his young plants first and the rest later. So too with
Meletus. He will perhaps first weed out those of us

3a   who blight the young shoots, as he claims; afterwards, he will obviously look after their elders
and become responsible for many great blessings
to the City, the natural result of so fine a beginning.

     E. I would hope so, Socrates, but I shudder for fear lest
the opposite may happen. He seems, as it were, to
be injuring the City from the start at its very

16

hearth,[1] in undertaking to wrong you. But tell me, what is it he says you do to corrupt the youth?

b   *S.* It sounds a bit strange at first hearing, my friend. He says I am a maker of gods, and on the ground that I make new ones, and do not worship the old ones, he indicted me on their account, he says.

  E. I see, Socrates. It is because you say the divine sign comes to you from time to time.[2] So he has indicted you for making innovations in religious matters, and hales you into court to slander you, knowing full well that such things are easily misrepresented to the multitude. Why I, even me,

c   when I speak about religious matters in the Assembly, foretelling the future to them, why, they laugh at me as though I were mad. And yet nothing I ever predicted has failed to come true. Still, they are jealous of people like us. We must not worry about them, but face them boldly.

  S. My dear Euthyphro, being laughed at is perhaps a thing of little moment. The Athenians, it seems to me, do not much care if they think a man is clever, so long as they do not suspect him of teaching his cleverness to others; but if they think he makes others like himself, they become angry, whether out

d   of jealousy as you suggest, or for some other reason.

  E. On that point I am not very anxious to test their attitude toward me.

  S. Perhaps they think you give yourself sparingly, that you are unwilling to teach your wisdom. But I fear my own generosity is such that they think me willing to pour myself out in speech to any man – not only without pay, but glad to pay myself if only someone will listen. So as I just said, if they were to laugh at me as you say they do you, it would not

e   be unpleasant to pass the time in court laughing

---

[1] 'As every home had its sacred hearth, so . . . had every town, situated in the building where the governing body had its seat, and where its members assembled for their common meal . . . On the hearth burned the sacred fire of the state', M. P. Nilsson, *History of Greek Religion* (2nd ed.), p. 127.

[2] 'It has come to me from my youth, a sort of voice, and when it comes it never urges me forward, but turns me back from what I am about to do.' *Apology*, 31d; cf. 40a–b.

17

and joking. But if they are in earnest, how it will then turn out is unclear – except to you prophets.

E. Perhaps it will not amount to much, Socrates. Perhaps you will settle your case satisfactorily, as I think I will mine.

S. What about that, Euthyphro? Are you plaintiff or defendant?

E. Plaintiff.

S. Against whom?

4a E. Someone I am again thought mad to prosecute.

S. Really? He has taken flight?

E. Far from flying. As a matter of fact, he is well along in years.

S. Who is he?

E. My father.

S. Your own father, dear friend?

E. Yes, indeed.

S. But what is the charge? What is the reason for the suit?

E. Murder, Socrates.

S. Heracles! Surely, Euthyphro, the majority of people must be ignorant of what is right. Not just anyone would undertake a thing like that. It must require
b someone quite far gone in wisdom.

E. By Zeus, very far indeed, Socrates.

S. Was the man your father killed a relative? But, of course, he must have been – you would not be prosecuting him for murder in behalf of a stranger.

E. It is laughable, Socrates, your thinking it makes a difference whether the man was a relative or not; the only thing to watch out for is whether his slayer was justified. If so, let him off. If not, prosecute him, even if he shares your hearth and table.
c For if you knowingly associate with a man like that and do not cleanse yourself, and him, by bringing action at law, the pollution is equal for you both. Now as a matter of fact, the dead man was a day-labourer of mine, and when we were farming in Naxos he worked for us for hire. Well, he got drunk and flew into a rage with one of our slaves and cut his throat. So my father bound him hand and foot, threw him in a ditch, and sent a man here to Athens to consult the religious adviser[1] as to

[1] The Exegete, charged with interpretation of religious law especially with regard to ritual propriety and special purifications for homicide. Little is known of the

18

what should be done. In the meantime, my father
d   paid no attention to the man he had bound; he
neglected him because he was a murderer and it
made no difference if he died. Which is just what
he did. He died of hunger and cold and his bonds
before the messenger got back. But even so, my
father and the rest of my relatives are angry at me
for prosecuting him for murder in behalf of a
murderer. For he did not kill him, they claim, and
even if he did, still, the fellow was a murderer, and
it is wrong to be concerned in behalf of a man like
that – and anyway, it is unholy for a son to prose-
e   cute his father for murder. They little know,
Socrates, how things stand in religious matters
regarding the holy and the unholy.

S. But in the name of Zeus, Euthyphro, do you think you
know so accurately how matters stand respecting
divine law, and things holy and unholy, that with
the facts as you declare, you can prosecute your
father without fear that it is you, on the contrary,
who are doing an unholy thing?

E. I would not be much use, Socrates, nor would Euthyphro differ in any way from the majority of men, if
5a   I did not know all such things with strict accuracy.

S. Well then, my gifted friend, I had best become your
pupil. Before the action with Meletus begins I will
challenge him on these very grounds. I will say
that even in former times I was much concerned to
learn about religious matters, but that now, in view
of his claiming that I am guilty of loose speech and
innovation in these things, I have become your
pupil. 'And if, Meletus,' I shall say, 'if you agree
that Euthyphro is wise in such things, then accept
b   the fact that I worship correctly and drop the case.
But if you do not agree, then obtain permission to
indict this my teacher in my place, for corrupting
the old – me and his own father – by teaching me,

---

precise nature of this office in the fifth century; its holders are referred to in the
plural at 9a. Plato made provision for the office in the *Laws* (VI, 759c–d): its holders
are charged among other things, with declaring what purifications shall be required
of those who murder slaves (*Laws*, IX 865c–d; cf. XI, 916c). For further discussion,
see W. K. C. Guthrie, *The Greeks and Their Gods*, pp. 186–8, and Glenn R. Morrow,
Plato's Cretan City, pp. 419–22.

and by correcting and punishing him.' And if I
can not persuade him to drop charges, or indict you
in place of me, might I not then say the same thing
in court I said in my challenge?

E. By Zeus, if he tried to indict me, I would find his weak
c   spot, I think, and the discussion in court would
concern him long before it concerned me.

S. I realize that, my friend. That is why I want to become
your pupil.

Of Euthyphro, we know little more than we are here told. He
seems to be fairly young (12a), though he has spoken often in the
Assembly, and his father is old. He is a seer.[1] He is an Athenian.
He does not have good sense. Since he is mentioned in the *Cratylus*
no less than five times as the source of the divine inspiration
which enables Socrates so skilfully to analyse names, and especially names of the gods, he is presumably also something of a
religious linguist.

The story here told of his suit is generally thought to have a
basis in fact, on the ground, often excellent in history, that it is
too good not to be true. Had he actually succeeded in convicting
his father, the old man would have been exiled; but it is unlikely
that Euthyphro could have won his case, or perhaps even have
tried it.

In the first place, Euthyphro's prosecution appears to be mistaken in law. Homicide, in Athens, differed from impiety in that
it was not a crime against the State, and therefore not prosecuted
under a γραφή or public indictment; it was treated as we treat
negligent damage, as a private wrong actionable by δίκη or civil
suit.[2] Ordinarily, for such an action to lie, plaintiff had to show tort
or personal injury under the law, and for that reason only the
family of a murdered freeman or, if a slave, the owner, was en-
titled to sue. Euthyphro, if he expected to find a ground in tort
for prosecuting his father in behalf of a hired man, had got things
precisely backwards. Since nothing now known of Attic law
indicates that an employer could serve as a plaintiff in such cases,

---

[1] An inaccurate one, as 3e implies. 'It is the seer's business to know the signs of
what is to come, death or disease or loss of property, victory or defeat in war or any
other struggle' (*Laches*, 195e–196a).

[2] For an account of this point, and its application in Athenian criminal law, see
Paul Vinogradoff, *Outlines of Historical Jurisprudence*, vol. ii, pp. 165 ff.

it is possible that the King in preliminary hearings refused to bring the suit to trial.[1]

Special rules applied when the murdered man was a foreigner without kinsmen in the city. It was then open to any citizen to prosecute, since murder, though a private wrong, produced blood-guilt and pollution, and the contagion of pollution was a matter affecting the public good.[2] Because the man his father killed was apparently a Naxian, not an Athenian, Euthyphro may have undertaken to use this provision of the law to bring his suit. But the killing occurred in Naxos, and Naxos had, for five years past, been foreign soil.[3] It is questionable, therefore, that an Athenian court would have claimed jurisdiction.

Questions of law apart, there are questions of fact. It is not explicitly said that the murderer of the slave was taken in the act, though Euthyphro's description suggests this. If that were so, Euthyphro's father had the legal right to execute the murderer on the spot; sending to the Exegete for instruction under these circumstances was an act of unusual scrupulousness. Perhaps,

---

[1] If indeed matters went as far as the preliminary hearing; the conclusion of the dialogue (15e) suggests that Euthyphro may have dropped charges after his talk with Socrates.

[2] See G. R. Morrow, *op. cit.*, pp. 274-5.

[3] Euthyphro and his father were presumably Athenian cleruchs in Naxos, and would have lost their holdings there in 404 B.C., when Athens' power over Naxos ended after Aegospotami. If so, then Euthyphro is bringing his suit five years after the fact, and common sense, if not a statute of limitations, would make against his case. If, on the other hand, Euthyphro and his father did not lose their holdings, and the killing was more recent, an Athenian court would have had no jurisdiction; the killing would have occurred on foreign soil, and probably involved a foreigner. This perhaps explains why Euthyphro stresses so strongly the dangers of pollution involved in allowing his father to go unpunished (4b-c). Only on the ground – legal niceties apart – that his father's unexpiated guilt was a threat to the citizenry could he have hoped to bring his case to trial in an Athenian court. Cf. W. A. Heidel, *Plato's Euthyphro*, p. 43.

There have been other explanations of the time-lapse. Schanz suggested that Plato is here committing a deliberate anachronism; but anachronism in the dialogues, though it occurs, is rare and generally intentional, and there is no sufficient reason for explaining its occurrence here. Alternately, Burnet suggested (on 4c, 4) that the crime took place in 404, but was not tried until 399 because Athenian constitutional revision between 403 and 401 delayed the administration of justice; but this is militated against by Aristotle's testimony (*Ath. Resp.*, 39, 5), and is intrinsically improbable; no society can safely suspend the administration of criminal justice, especially in matters of homicide, for so long a period.

however, the very fact that instruction was sought indicates that the murderer was not taken in the act. Still, his guilt must have been certain, since even Euthyphro, appearing in his behalf, does not question it. No doubt it is unwise to predict the verdict of any jury, and certainly Euthyphro's father, by present-day standards, was guilty at the very least of callous disregard – manslaughter, if not murder. But this rests in good part on a developed concept of due process of law, alien to Greece, in terms of which even a murderer taken in the act has a right to a trial; Greek law was closer to the code of the blood-feud in these matters, and more direct. This explains why, if I have heard correctly the tone of voice at 9a (cf. 15d), Socrates himself doubted that Euthyphro's father was guilty of homicide. An Athenian jury would have been likely to hold that if a drunken murderer, rightly apprehended and bound by the owner of the slave he had killed, was so unreasonable as to die of exposure while due and proper advice was being sought from accredited religious authority, he did so on his own responsibility.

Euthyphro, himself an authority on religious matters, thinks otherwise. Confident that pollution exists, he is prosecuting to clear it both from his father and himself (4e), and he expects his suit to be brought to a satisfactory conclusion (3e). That is, he expects his father to be convicted and exiled. There is no ground whatever for supposing that he filed his suit expecting it to be dismissed, in the belief that he would then have done 'all that a scrupulous conscience can require'.[1] Pollution was not a matter of conscience, however scrupulous; its contagion was real, as independent of human moral judgement or human regret as the contagion of any disease. And like a disease, it required its own peculiar pharmacy.

The primary question raised by Plato's introduction to the *Euthyphro* is not whether Euthyphro's action is right, but how we are to determine whether his action is right. Euthyphro is prosecuting his father on the ground that it is pious or holy to do so. But the ancient family was knit beyond natural affection by the engrained sanctions of religious law, and to Euthyphro's father, his relations, and most ordinary Athenians such a prosecution, lodged in the name of piety, would have seemed a thing most

[1] As A. E. Taylor suggested, *Plato*, p. 147.

monstrously impious. When moral opinions are in conflict, how is their truth to be judged? The introduction to the *Euthyphro* is meant to exhibit a need which the dialogue will later explicitly state: the need for a standard by which to determine what things are genuinely holy and what are not. That standard, it will appear, is the essential nature, or Form, of holiness.

This fact makes debate over Euthyphro's character irrelevant. The name Euthyphro, etymologically, means Straight-thinker, or, as an adjective, 'sincere', and some modern readers have wondered whether Euthyphro's thinking was not considerably straighter, and his action considerably more sincere, than Plato's ironical picture of him allows. Without entering on useless debate, it may be remarked that so far as the text is concerned, Euthyphro's motive in launching his suit was not a desire for even-handed justice, or retribution for cruelty, or pity for the helpless and oppressed; it was a desire to avoid pollution, and thus very like desire to avoid catching the plague. This is the motive, and it is the only motive, which Euthyphro avows for his action (4b–c). To some degree, certainly, it is an unselfish motive, in that Euthyphro wishes not only to avoid contagion himself, but to see his father cleansed. So much for the ties of kinship. But a sensible man, before proceeding in such a cause, might be expected to have acquired clear knowledge that pollution existed – that is, that under the given circumstances, Euthyphro's father's action was homicide. That question, which in Greek law was open to reasonable doubt, is one which Euthyphro settles by appeal to special authority – namely, his own as an expert in religious matters. Euthyphro's indictment of his father, then, like Meletus' indictment of Socrates, raises a problem of knowledge. Opinions differ on questions of piety and impiety. How are we to get at the truth? Given Euthyphro's confident, almost touching, belief that he knows 'how matters stand respecting divine law, and things holy and unholy' (4e), it is not surprising that Socrates, who knows only that he does not know, and has some reason for curiosity in matters touching piety and religion, should offer forthwith to become his pupil.

2. THE REQUEST FOR A DEFINITION (5C–6E)

Having volunteered to *Euthyphro* for instruction, Socrates undertakes to obtain it by asking what the holy or the pious is. In the remainder of the dialogue he will examine and refute a series of replies. The examination proceeds by question and answer, a technique of discussion to which Plato later gave the name of 'dialectic', a word whose ordinary meaning was simply conversation, but here suggests conversation of a rather special kind.

Euthyphro will first say that the holy is just what he is now doing, prosecuting his father for murder. Given his peculiar convictions, he is perhaps not to be blamed for his reply: throughout the early dialogues, Socrates' respondents, when first asked the meaning of a moral term, give examples of it – examples which also reveal their character – and it sometimes takes considerable effort to convince them that this is not what is required. Laches, a soldier, will say that courage is sticking to your post and not running away in the face of the enemy (*Laches*, 190e). Charmides, a sought-after youth, thinks that temperance is keeping quiet and being modest (*Charmides*, 159b). Cephalus, an elderly businessman, will say that justice is telling the truth and paying your debts (*Republic*, I, 331b). And Hippias, a Sophist who apparently had other interests, thinks that the beautiful is a beautiful maiden, though he later hazards the guess that it is gold (*Hippias Major*, 287e, 289e).

Part of the difficulty lay in the novelty of the question: Socrates, as Aristotle implied, was the first man in history to seek definitions of moral terms in ordinary language from ordinary men. But part of the difficulty lay too in the fact that the Socratic question, baldly put, admitted of very different sorts of answers.

Expressions such as τὸ ὅσιον, 'the holy', τὸ καλόν, 'the beautiful', or τὸ δίκαιον, 'the just' – such terms as Socrates commonly used in formulating his peculiar questions – are ambiguous. They are constructed from neuter singular adjectives with agreeing article, and they function in three different ways: as singular referring expressions, as generic nouns, and as abstract nouns. In some contexts, τὸ ὅσιον may refer to some particular holy thing under discussion. In others it may be used generically, with the singular then equivalent to a plural, τὸ ὅσιον, 'the holy', equivalent to τὰ ὅσια, 'holy things'; those holy things may be individuals which are holy, taken collectively or distributively, or kinds of individuals which are holy. Finally, τὸ ὅσιον may be used as an abstract noun, equivalent in meaning to 'holiness', ὁσιότης.

It is not therefore surprising, given the ambiguity of the

question, 'What is τὸ ὅσιον?', that Euthyphro should undertake to say what holiness is by giving examples of it, even though Socrates, in asking his question, works to make his meaning clear. Socrates will ask what the holy itself is in itself, and whether it is not the same in every holy action, and whether everything which is to be unholy does not have a single character (5d). Euthyphro will reply with his example: the holy is doing just what he is doing now, prosecuting murderers and temple thieves. Specifically, his own action in prosecuting his father is holy, a thing proved by egregious theological precedent: he is doing no more than Zeus himself did to his own father, and that father to his father before him.[1]

Euthyphro's notions of divinity derive from Hesiod and Homer; his confidence in them would hardly have been shared by educated Athenians of his time. As Xenophanes[2] had pointed out a century earlier, 'Homer and Hesiod have ascribed to the gods all things that are a shame and a disgrace among mortals, stealings and adulteries and deceivings of one another.' Reflective men in the late fifth century were reluctant to ascribe to deity vices they condemned in themselves. The bloody history of Zeus, Cronos, and Uranus was generally treated as allegory, or frankly dismissed as false. Euthyphro thinks otherwise.

The word here rendered as 'holy', ὅσιον, admits of no precise translation; neither does εὐσεβές, 'pious', used here as a synonym. Holiness, in English, is primarily an attribute of divinity or of sacred objects associated with worship. But the primary meaning of ὅσιον is 'sanctioned by divine law', often in contrast to human law; Euthyphro, if his case was dismissed, doubtless felt the incongruence. What is ὅσιον is religiously required, or religiously permissible,[3] or ritually clean, whence the opposite, ἀνόσιον, has often very nearly the force of 'tabu' or 'polluted'. Ὅσιον also differs from 'holy' in its application to persons. A holy man in English is likely to be someone who dines off acorns. But in Greek

---

[1] It is worth remarking that this comparison of his own case to that of Zeus would have struck the average Athenian as a breath-taking display of *hubris* – and impiety.

[2] *DK*, Fr. 11, trans. Burnet.

[3] This leads to a curiosity of language: because ὅσιον could mean religiously permitted, it came to have the meaning of 'profane', as what is not forbidden by divine law. The word is so used in the phrase ἱερὰ καὶ ὅσια, 'things sacred and profane' (see *LSJ*, ὅσιον, I.2.) But it is not generally so used without its defining opposite, and in the *Euthyphro*, ὅσιον is equivalent to εὐσεβές, which does not admit this use at all.

ὁσιότης is a traditional moral excellence, closely associated with justice, and indeed the religious aspect of justice.[1] The noun ἡ ὁσία may mean divine law, or the services owed the gods in rites and offerings. Euthyphro, in his efforts to provide Socrates with instruction, will appeal to several of these senses to make his meaning clear.

> *(Socrates continues)* I know that this fellow Meletus, and no doubt other people too,[2] pretend not even to notice you; but he saw through me so keenly and easily that he indicted me for impiety. So now in Zeus's name, tell me what you confidently claimed just now that you knew: what sort of thing do you say the pious and impious are, both
>
> d with respect to murder and other things as well? Or is not the holy, itself by itself, the same in every action? And the unholy, in turn, the opposite of all the holy – is it not like itself, and does not everything which is to be unholy have a certain single character with respect to unholiness?

E. No doubt, Socrates.

S. Then tell me, what do you say the holy is? And what is the unholy?

E. Well, I say that the holy is just what I am doing now, prosecuting murder and temple theft and everything of the sort, whether it is a father or mother

e or anyone else who is guilty of it. And not prosecuting is unholy. Now, Socrates, examine the proof I shall give you that this is a dictate of divine law. I have offered it before to other people, to show that it is established right not to let off someone guilty of impiety, no matter who he happens to be. For these same people worship Zeus as the best and most righteous of the gods. And they

6a agree that he put his own father in bonds for swallowing his children unjustly; yes, and that that father had in his turn castrated his father, for similar reasons. Yet me they are angry at for indicting my father for his injustice. So they contradict themselves: they say one thing about the gods and another about me.

---

[1] For further discussion, see A. W. H. Adkins, *Merit and Responsibility*, pp. 132–8.
[2] ἄλλος . . . τις, singular for plural; cf. *Apology*, 30d, 3.

S. I wonder if this is why I am being prosecuted, Euthyphro, because when anyone says such things about the gods, I somehow find it difficult to accept? Perhaps that is why people will claim I transgress. But as it is, if even you who know such things so
b   well accept them, people like me must apparently concede. What indeed are we to say, we who ourselves agree that we know nothing of them. But in the name of Zeus, the God of Friendship, tell me: do you truly believe that these things happened so?[1]

E. Yes, and things still more wonderful than these, Socrates, which the multitude does not know.

S. Do you believe there is really war among the gods, and terrible enmities, and battles, and other things of the sort our poets tell, which embellish other things sacred to us through the work of our capable
c   painters, but especially embellish the robe filled with embroidery that is carried to the Acropolis at the Great Panathenaea? Are we, Euthyphro, to say those things are so?

E. Not only those, Socrates. As I just said, I shall explain many other things about religion to you if you wish, and you may rest assured that what you hear will amaze you.

S. I should not be surprised. But explain them another time at your leisure; right now, try to answer more
d   clearly the question I just asked. For, my friend, you did not sufficiently teach me before, when I asked you what the holy is: you said that the thing you are doing now is holy, prosecuting your father for murder.

E. Yes, and I told the truth, Socrates.

S. Perhaps. But, Euthyphro, are there not many other things you say are holy too?

E. Of course there are.

S. Do you recall that I did not ask you to teach me about some one or two of the many things which are holy, but about that characteristic itself by which all holy things are holy? For you agreed, I think, that it is by one character that unholy

---

[1] The irony of this remark is not diminished by the fact that Zeus was also god of kinship or blood-relation, and the 'Purifier', expiator of blood-guilt.

e   things are unholy and holy things holy. Or do you not recall?

E. I do.

S. Then teach me what this same character is, so that I may look to it and use it as a standard, which, should those things which you or someone else may do be of that sort, I may affirm that they are holy, but should they not be of that sort, deny it.

E. Well if you wish it so, Socrates, so shall I tell you.

S. I do indeed wish it.

Socrates has progressively specified the nature of his question. He begins by remarking, mildly enough under the circumstances, that for Euthyphro to undertake his suit, he must think he knows accurately, 'how matters stand respecting divine law, and things holy and unholy'. He next proceeds to ask what the holy is, and puts his question with considerable precision, explaining that the holy must be holy 'itself by itself' – that is, holiness as such, and the same in every action, a single character which anything which is to be holy must have. When Euthyphro supplies examples rather than a definition, Socrates proceeds to make his question more specific still. Other things are holy besides prosecuting murderers and temple thieves, and Socrates wishes to be taught the nature of the characteristic itself by which holy things are holy, so that he may use it as a standard to determine what actions are holy and what are not (6d–e). He wishes, in short, to be told the nature of a universal, and he expects to use that universal as a standard for determining whether any given action – say, Euthyphro's in prosecuting his father – is holy. Though Euthyphro thinks he understands this question, his answers will show that he does not.

The words ἰδέα (5d, 6d, e) and εἶδος (6d), here rendered neutrally as 'character' and 'characteristic', are used in this context as synonyms, and their use is technical. Both derive from the root *Ϝιδ, which appears in common Greek verbs for seeing and knowing, in Latin *videre*, German *wissen*, and English 'wise' and 'wit'. Their meaning appears originally to have been associated with the 'look' of a thing, its *species* or outward appearance; they were used by pre-Platonic mathematicians to mean figure, shape, or pattern, and in a parallel use they meant the human figure, the human shape.[1] In the medical writers, εἶδος meant 'constitution', or the sort or kind of a disease. Thucydides speaks of death in every ἰδέα, every form, and a mask in Euripides uses the word to ask the nature of something, what sort of thing it is.[2]

The ordinary meaning of 'sort' or 'kind' is a common one in Plato; but the words are here used in a special way. The εἶδος or ἰδέα is a universal, the same in all its instances and something the instances *have* (5d); it is in some sense a condition for the existence of holy things, that *by* which – the dative is instrumental – holy things are holy; and it is a standard or παράδειγμα for determining what things are holy and what are not. In short, the words εἶδος and ἰδέα here carry freight they do not ordinarily bear, and for that reason commentators have often translated them as 'Idea' or 'Form'. The latter is preferable. 'Idea' has the advantage of closer relation to the Greek; but Locke, who first introduced the word into English philosophy, also gave it a subjective and psychological connotation it has never since lost. Etymologically, this is perhaps in some ways commendable. As a translation of what is here meant, it is misleading.

Socrates' question, 'What is the holy?', then, is the question, 'What is the Form of holiness?' The notion of Form here involved will guide the dialectic throughout the remainder of the dialogue.

3. FIRST DEFINITION: THE HOLY, WHAT IS LOVED BY THE GODS (6E–8B)

Euthyphro now abandons his attempt to say what the holy is by offering examples, and suggests a formula: the holy is what is loved by the gods.

This formula escapes a principal defect of his first attempt: it provides a distinguishing mark, setting off, at least in intention, all those and only those things which are to be holy. The requirement of universality has now been met. But the definition proceeds in a sense by example still: it specifies a group of individuals – things, actions, persons (7a) – marked off from the rest by being loved by

---

[1] And are so used by Plato at *Charmides*, 154d, 158a, *Protagoras*, 352a.

[2] For further discussion, see Burnet, *op. cit.*, on 5d, 3; A. E. Taylor, *Varia Socratica*, pp. 178–267; C. M. Gillespie, *Classical Quarterly*, vi (1912), pp. 179–203. For Presocratic uses, see Diels-Kranz, *Die Fragmente der Vorsokratiker*, vol. iii (8th ed.). R. S. Bluck, *Plato's* Meno, pp. 224–5, gives further references.

the gods. And it is the individuals, not their distinguishing mark, which are identified with the holy.

7a

E. Then what is dear to the gods is holy, and what is not dear to them is unholy.

S. Excellent, Euthyphro. You have now answered as I asked you to. Whether correctly, I do not yet know – but clearly you will now go on to teach me that what you say is true.

E. Of course.

S. Come then, let us examine what it is we are saying. The thing and the person dear to the gods is holy; the thing and the person hateful to the gods is unholy; and the holy is not the same as the unholy, but its utter opposite. Is that what we are saying?

E. It is.

S. Yes, and is it also well said?

b

E. I think so, Socrates.

S. Now, Euthyphro, we also said, did we not, that the gods quarrel and disagree with one another, and that there is enmity among them?

E. We did.

S. But what is the disagreement which causes enmity and anger about, my friend? Look at it this way: If you and I were to disagree about a question of number, about which of two sums is greater, would our disagreement cause us to become angry with each other and make us enemies? Or would we take to

c

counting in a case like that, and quickly settle our dispute?

E. Of course we would.

S. So too, if we disagreed about a question of the larger and smaller, we would take to measurement, and put an end to our disagreement quickly?

E. True.

S. And we would go to the balance, I imagine, to settle a dispute about the heavier and lighter?

E. Certainly.

S. But what sort of thing would make us enemies, angry at each other, if we disagreed about it and were unable to arrive at a decision? Perhaps you cannot

d

say offhand, but I suggest you consider whether it would not be the just and the unjust, beautiful and ugly, good and evil. Is it not these things, when we disagree about them, and cannot reach a satisfactory decision, concerning which we on occasion become enemies – you, and I, and all other men?

E. Yes, Socrates. This kind of disagreement has its source there.

S. What about the gods, Euthyphro? If they were to disagree, would they not disagree for the same reasons?

E. Necessarily.

e S. Then by your account, my noble friend, different gods must believe that different things are just – and beautiful and ugly, good and evil. For surely they would not quarrel unless they disagreed on this. True?

E. You are right.

S. Now, what each of them believes to be beautiful and good and just they also love, and the opposites of those things they hate?

E. Of course.

S. Yes, but the same things, you say, are thought by some gods to be just and by others unjust. Those are the

8a things concerning which disagreement causes them to quarrel and make war on one another. True?

E. Yes.

S. Then the same things, it seems, are both hated by the gods and loved by the gods, and would be both dear to the gods and hateful to the gods.

E. It seems so.

S. Then by this account, Euthyphro, the same things would be both holy and unholy.

E. I suppose so.

S. Then you have not answered my question, my friend. I did not ask you what same thing happens to be both holy and unholy; yet what is dear to the gods is hateful to the gods, it seems. And so, Euthyphro,

b it would not be surprising if what you are now doing in punishing your father were dear to Zeus, but hateful to Cronos and Uranus, and loved by Hephaestus, but hateful to Hera; and if any of the other gods disagree about it, the same will be true of them too.

Socrates begins his examination by making Euthyphro's formula more precise: what is dear to the gods (προσφιλές) is holy; what is hateful to the gods (θεομισές) is unholy; and the holy is not the same as the unholy, but its utter opposite.

He next recalls Euthyphro's earlier claim that the gods disagree among themselves, and that their disagreement causes anger and enmity. Over what sort of thing will such enmity arise?

Socrates answers with an implicit division. There are two kinds of disagreement among men: those which cause enmity and those which do not. Those which do not cause enmity admit of satisfactory decision (ἱκανὴν κρίσιν), which is obtained by recourse to such independent procedures as counting, weighing, and measuring.[1] Those which cause enmity admit of no satisfactory decision, and they arise over questions of justice and injustice, beauty and ugliness or nobility and shamefulness, and good and evil.[2] Euthyphro readily admits that, as with men, so too with gods. If there is enmity among the gods, they also must disagree in these matters.

It will be observed that this argument is not demonstrative, but dialectical, 'making use of those things which the respondent agrees that he knows' (*Meno*, 75d). The discussion proceeds from Euthyphro's own admissions; its conclusion is drawn by analogy; its premises are established by examples or by simple appeal to obviousness.

It has been thought that the point of this argument is to distinguish 'factual' questions, for which there is a decision procedure, from 'moral' questions, for which there is none. The division may then be attacked on the ground that not all factual questions are decidable by a procedure, and not all moral questions are undecidable.[3] But the argument attempts nothing so grand. Its aim is to analyse the nature of disagreement which causes anger and enmity. To this end, it distinguishes the subject-matter *about* which enmity arises, and the situation *in* which it arises. The subject-matter involves, broadly, questions of worth or value; the situation, lack of a satisfactory procedure for settling those questions. It is assumed that where enmity is present, both of these conditions will be present. This is not equivalent to assuming that all questions of worth or value lack satisfactory procedures for decision, or that all 'factual' questions admit such procedures. Nor is it equivalent to assuming a rigid contrast between 'fact'

[1] Cf. *Protagoras*, 356c–357c.
[2] Cf. *Alcibiades*, I, 112a–c; compare Euripides, *Phoenissae*, 499–502.
[3] Cf. P. T. Geach, *Monist*, 50 (1966), pp. 373–4.

and 'value'; it gives no ground for supposing that, in any ordinary sense, the question of whether Euthyphro's prosecution is pious or holy, say, is not a question of fact.

There is a further point. The argument traces enmity to disagreements which have not admitted of satisfactory decision; but it neither suggests nor implies that such disagreements admit of no satisfactory decision *in principle*. Socrates, on the contrary, would have supposed that they admit of decision: his purpose in requesting a definition of holiness was to gain knowledge of a standard which would provide certainty of judgement in disputed cases: As Burnet pointed out, Forms are in moral matters what scales are to weight and yardsticks to length. Euthyphro's belief that the gods themselves can reach no satisfactory decision on such questions bodes ill for the success of his definition.

And so it proves. Socrates next elicits the admission that the gods love what they think just and noble and good, and hate what they think the opposite. Since their enmity implies that they disagree over which things are which, it follows that the same things are loved and hated by the gods. But if this is true, the holy is also unholy, whereas it had been agreed that the holy and the unholy are not the same, but utter opposites. The trap snaps shut.

It may well seem to have closed on thin air. Judged by the canons of definition to be found in any standard textbook of traditional logic,[1] this refutation seems beside the point. The definition has not been rejected because it does not state essence, though in fact it does not, as Euthyphro's attempt to amend it will show (11a). It has not been rejected because it is not expressed *per genus et differentiam*, though this too is one of its defects (11e–12a). The definition is not circular, or negative, or expressed in obscure or figurative language. Is it then rejected because it is too broad, because holiness is defined in such a way that holy things may also be unholy? If so, the refutation fails. No odd number is even; but some tall things are short – tall pygmies, for example – and Hippias' maiden, though beautiful, was ugly compared to a goddess.[2] It is not self-evidently false that some holy things are also unholy, and if Euthyphro's peculiar theology is sound, his definition implies that it is true.[3]

---

[1] See, for example, H. W. B. Joseph, *Introduction to Logic* (2nd ed.), pp. 111–15.

[2] *Hippias Major*, 289a–b.

[3] Mr Norman Gulley (*The Philosophy of Socrates*, pp. 53, 54) suggests that the

But this neglects the peculiar character of Socrates' question. Euthyphro's definition specifies a group of individuals set off from others by a distinguishing mark, that of being loved by the gods: 'the holy' is used to mean things which are holy. But Socrates had requested, not an account of things which are holy, but the definition of a Form of holiness, which should serve as a standard for determining which things are holy and which things are not; and we can scarcely identify a thing as holy by comparing it to things some of which are examples of the opposite of holiness. The difficulty, indeed, lies deeper. We cannot determine that those things to which we compare it are themselves either holy or unholy without knowledge of holiness and unholiness in and of themselves.[1] The reason, then, for rejecting Euthyphro's definition is that it cannot in principle provide a basis for sufficient decision in determining what things are holy and what things are not.[2]

The use of the Form as a standard provides the inner connection between Socrates' 'What is it?' question and his customary claim that moral excellence is somehow analogous to art, or that it is an art of using arts, or the goods pursued in other arts:[3]

> In short, Cleinias, all those things which we first called goods, . . . if they are guided by ignorance, are greater evils than their opposites, in as much as they are more able to minister to their evil guide. But if they are guided by wisdom and understanding, they are greater goods; and in themselves, they are of no value.

An art is a form of knowledge. The demand for moral science is found in many of the early dialogues, and is connected with the notion of a moral governor, someone whose skill or wisdom is such that he will stand to the mass of ordinary men in moral matters as the trainer stands to athletes, the physician to patients, the pilot to his crew – as fitted to govern because of knowledge. Such wisdom is not to be found in the Many, as analogy shows:

[1] Cf. H. F. Cherniss, 'The Philosophical Economy of the Theory of Ideas', *SPM*, pp. 2–3. To anticipate a bit, a distinguishing mark, such as being loved by the gods (some or all), is unreliable unless it is a statement of essence.

[2] For further discussion, see below, pp. 71-72.

[3] *Euthydemus*, 281d–e; cf. *Meno*, 87e–88d.

reason Euthyphro's definition is rejected is simply that, 'the possession of piety excludes the possession of its opposite, impiety' at 5d 1–5. But in fact, that passage neither states nor implies this, and to assume it in criticism of the definition Euthyphro has presented would be a straightforward *petitio*.

for the Many are not competent trainers or physicians or pilots. Yet those sorts of competence merely touch the body; how much more important is competence in matters of the soul:[1]

> Especially in matters of right and wrong, shame and nobility, good and evil – just the things we are now concerned with – are we to follow the judgement of the Many, and fear it, or is it the judgement of one man, if he but have knowledge, whom one ought to reverence and fear beyond all the rest?

Because Forms are standards, they provide a basis for moral science; this, then, is one source of the Socratic doctrine that Virtue is Knowledge.

4. FIRST INTERLUDE (8B–9C)

Socratic dialectic has a personal thrust, and Euthyphro senses it immediately. It is not only his definition, but the quality of his character and life that are under scrutiny. As Nicias remarks to Lysimachus in the *Laches* (187e ff.):

> I don't think you realize that anyone who has contact with Socrates and enters into conversation with him is necessarily drawn into argument; and whatever the subject he begins, he will continually be carried round and round until at last he finds that he has to give an account of his life, both past and present; and when he is once entangled, Socrates will not let him go until he has thoroughly and properly put all his ways to the test.

Euthyphro is learning what Nicias knew, and he will find it increasingly embarrassing. He cannot directly answer the peculiar objections Socrates has raised, but he sees where they tend, and his first thought is to defend his action. Perhaps the gods do disagree in their loves and hates; but surely, he thinks, they agree that a man who kills another man unjustly should be punished for it. This will lead directly to a second definition, that holiness is what *all* the gods love, and unholiness what they all hate. But it is irrelevant to the first definition: it is Euthyphro's justification for his peculiar prosecution.

Socrates easily exposes its weakness. Of course the gods agree that the man who kills another man unjustly should be punished. Who, after all, would not? But that is not the question. The question is: When is a killing unjust?

---

[1] *Crito*, 47c–d; cf. *Lysis*, 210b, *Alcibiades*, I, 111–112, *Laches*, 184d ff.

E. But Socrates, surely none of the gods disagree about this, that he who kills another man unjustly should answer for it.

c

S. Really, Euthyphro? Have you ever heard it argued among *men* that he who kills unjustly, or does anything else unjustly, should not answer for it?

E. Why, people never stop arguing things like that, especially in court. They do a host of wrongs, and then say and do everything to get off.

S. Yes, but do they admit the wrong, Euthyphro, and, admitting it, still claim that they should not answer for it?

E. No; they certainly do not do that.

S. Then they do not do and say everything: for they do not, I think, dare to contend that if they in fact did a wrong they should not answer for it. Rather, I think, they deny they did wrong. Well?

d

E. True.

S. So they do not contend that those who do wrong should not answer for it, but rather, perhaps, about who it is that did the wrong, and what he did, and when.

E. True.

S. Now is it not also the same with the gods, if, as your account has it, they quarrel about what is just and unjust, and some claim that others do wrong,[1] and some deny it? Presumably no one, god or man,

e

would dare to claim that he who does a wrong should not answer for it.

E. Yes, on the whole what you say is true, Socrates.

S. But I imagine that those who disagree, Euthyphro – both men and gods, if indeed the gods disagree – disagree about particular things which have been done. They differ over given actions, some claiming that these have been done justly, and others unjustly. True?

E. Certainly.

9a

S. Come now, my friend, teach me too and make me wiser. Where is your proof that all the gods believe that a man has been unjustly killed who, hired as a labourer, became a murderer, was bound by the master of the dead slave, and died of his bonds before the man

---

[1] Reading ἄλλους ἀδικεῖν for ἀλλήλους ἀδικεῖν. See W. A. Heidel, *Plato's* Euthyphro, p. 100.

b

who bound him could learn from the religious advisers what to do? Where is your proof that it is right for a son to indict and prosecute his father for murder in behalf of a man like that? Come, try to show me clearly that all the gods genuinely believe this action right. If you succeed, I shall praise you for your wisdom and never stop.

E. Well, I can certainly do it, Socrates, but it is perhaps not a small task.

S. I see. You think I am rather harder to teach than the judges; you will certainly make it clear to them that actions such as your father's are wrong, and that all the gods hate them.

E. Very clear indeed, Socrates, if they listen to what I say.

c

S. They will listen, if you seem to speak well.

The dialectic here once more brings the central problem of the *Euthyphro* into clear focus. Euthyphro is confident that it is right for him to prosecute his father: it is the holy thing to do, and the gods demand it. His father, his relatives, and most ordinary Athenians are equally confident that what he is doing is wrong. Where judgements are so sharply in conflict, how can a sufficient decision be reached?

Confidence is not knowledge, and without knowledge it is often misplaced.[1] If one is to know whether a given action is holy or not, one must learn the nature of holiness, a standard for satisfactory decision.[2] The search for a definition continues.

5. SECOND DEFINITION: THE HOLY, WHAT IS LOVED BY ALL THE GODS (9C–11A)

Dialectic is often progressive or genetic: new definitions grow out of what has gone before. And so it is here. Euthyphro's first definition foundered on the fact that the gods disagree in their loves and hates; but he remained convinced that all of them approve of prosecuting murderers, and this now leads to a revision: the holy is what is loved by *all* the gods.

Socrates' refutation of this second definition will apply with equal force to the first. For the root of the difficulty with Euthy-

---

[1] Cf. *Crito*, 46b.

[2] Cf. *Protagoras*, 360e–361a, *Republic*, I, 344d–e, *Laches*, 1900, *Hippias Major* 286c–e.

phro's first definition goes deeper than Socrates' refutation of it indicated: it is definition by distinguishing mark, rather than an analysis of essence, and the fault in this is now to be exposed.

Socrates begins his examination by asking whether the holy is loved by the gods because it is holy, or holy because it is loved. Euthyphro at first does not understand the question, and Socrates provides examples to explain what he means. Once Euthyphro has seen that there is a difference between carrying and being carried, leading, and being led, seeing and being seen, he realizes that there is a difference between loving and being loved, and what that difference is.

> (*Socrates continues*) Here is something that occurred to me while you were talking. I asked myself, 'Suppose Euthyphro were to teach me beyond any question that all the gods believe a death of this sort wrong. What more have I learned from Euthyphro about what the holy and the unholy are? The death, it seems, would be hateful to the gods. But what is holy and what is not proved, just now, not to be marked off by this; for what was hateful to the gods proved dear to the gods as well.' So I let you go on that point, Euthyphro: if you wish, let all the gods
>
> d   believe your father's action wrong, and let all of them hate it. But is this the correction we are now to make in your account, that what *all* the gods hate is unholy, and what *all* the gods love is holy, but what some love and some hate is neither or both? Do you mean for us now to mark off the holy and the unholy in that way?
>
> E. What is to prevent it, Socrates?
>
> S. Nothing, at least as far as I am concerned, Euthyphro. But, examine your account to see whether, if you assume this, you will most easily teach me what you promised.
>
> e   E. But I would certainly say that the holy is what all the gods love, and that the opposite, what all the gods hate, is unholy.
>
> S. Well, Euthyphro, should we examine this in turn to see if it is true? Or should we let it go, accept it from ourselves or anyone else without more ado, and agree that a thing is so if only someone says it is? Should we consider what he who says this means?

E. Of course. I believe, though, that this time what I say is true.

10a *S.* Perhaps we shall learn better, my friend. For consider: is the holy loved by the gods because it is holy? Or is it holy because it is loved by the gods?

E. I do not know what you mean, Socrates.

S. Then I will try to put it more clearly. We speak of carrying and being carried, of leading and being led, of seeing and being seen. And you understand in such cases, do you not, that they differ from each other, and how they differ?

E. Yes; I think I do.

S. Now, is there such a thing as being loved, and is it different from loving?

E. Of course.

b *S.* Then tell me: if a thing is being carried, is it being carried because of the carrying, or for some other reason?

E. No, for that reason.

S. And if a thing is being led, it is being led because of the leading? And if being seen, being seen because of the seeing?

E. Certainly.

S. Then it is not because a thing is being seen that the seeing exists; on the contrary, it is because of the seeing that it is being seen. Nor is it because a thing is being led that the leading exists; it is because of the leading that it is being led. Nor is it because a thing is being carried that the carrying exists; it is because of the carrying that it is being carried. Is

c what I mean quite clear, Euthyphro? I mean this: if something comes to be or something is affected in a certain way, it is not because it is a thing which is coming to be that the process of coming to be exists, but, because of the process of coming to be, it is a thing which is coming to be; it is not because it is affected that the affecting exists, but because of the affecting, the thing is affected. Do you agree?

E. Yes.

S. Now, if a thing is being loved, it is either something which is coming to be or something which is affected by something.

39

E. Of course.

S. And so it is as true of this as it was of the former: it is not because a thing is being loved that there is loving by those who love it; it is because of the loving that it is being loved.

E. Necessarily.

The point of this argument may well seem nearly opaque, an impression which commentators who believe that Socrates is here exploring the mysteries of active and passive voice have done little to correct. Active and passive are symmetrical: if the farmer milks the cow, the cow is milked by the farmer. And this symmetry holds when we desert grammar for the more abstract language of formal logic, and speak of the domain and converse domain of the relation 'milks' – the lactative relation, one assumes. But Socrates is here concerned, not with a symmetry, but with an asymmetry: a thing being carried is being carried because of the carrying; the carrying does not exist because the thing is being carried. The language of his examples is in fact cast, not into a contrast between active and passive forms of the verb, but into passive participle and corresponding passive verb, a feature of the Greek which cannot without undue clumsiness be preserved in translation.

Socrates' purpose is neither logical nor linguistic: he means to exhibit a priority in the structure of facts. Specifically, he is concerned to show that carrying is prior to being carried, leading prior to being led, seeing prior to being seen, and that, therefore, loving is prior to being loved. The priority involved is not temporal, but conditional: there are activities, such as carrying, and there are counterpart properties engendered by those activities, such as being carried; the counterpart properties exist because of the activities, but the activities do not exist because of the counterpart properties.[1] This point is sometimes confused with a very different one. Activities generally require objects.[2] To milk a cow, you must have a cow, so the cow is a condition of the milking. But

---

[1] There are, of course, various kinds of activities; carrying implies physical alternation, and so, at least in some cases, does leading; seeing and loving do not. So loving and carrying are not in this respect analogous. They are rather analogous as species of the same genus. Both are activities. They are prior to being loved and being carried as activities and prior to their objects *as* objects of them. Cf. *Gorgias* 476.

[2] Cf. *Charmides*, 167d ff.

to have a milked cow you must milk her, so the milking is a condition of the counterpart property in the cow of being milked.

The pattern of Socrates' argument is one made familiar by many early dialogues.[1] Three examples are offered here: carrying and being carried, leading and being led, seeing and being seen. Inspection of examples brings to light an identical relation in each of them: here, the priority of action to counterpart properties produced by action. This relation is then stated as a general rule, holding for anything that comes to be or is affected by something. It is then agreed that loving and being loved satisfy the conditions of the rule, from which it follows that they fall under the rule: 'It is not because a thing is being loved that there is loving by those who love it; it is because of the loving that it is being loved' (10c).

The final movement of this pattern of argument, from general rule to specific application, is deductive.[2] The initial movement, from a set of examples to a general rule, is 'induction', to use Aristotle's language, an ἐπαγωγή or 'leading on' from particulars to a universal. Plato in later life called it Example (παράδειγμα), and in the *Politicus* (277d–278e) explained the nature of Example by example.

Take children just learning to read – that is, learning to read as the ancients did, aloud. They know the letters of the alphabet, and recognize short and easy syllables. But they make mistakes. The best way to correct those mistakes is to lead them (ἀνάγειν, ἐπάγειν) to words they know, and then to set beside those words other words which they do not know, but which have similar combinations of letters. In this way, children learn to recognize sameness of relation in different contexts, and their skill in reading improves.

As with books, so with the book of nature. The example exhibits the nature of Example: 'An example is produced when what is the same in different and unconnected contexts is compared and rightly judged to apply in each, so that the two together complete a single true judgement' (*Politicus*, 278c). The method of example is a means of recognizing identity in difference. At bottom, it is

[1] For similar specimens of argument, see *Charmides*, 159c–160b, *Apology*, 27b–c, *Euthydemus*, 279c–280a, *Laches*, 192e–193d, *Protagoras*, 349e–350c. This list is not exhaustive.

[2] Though in many cases the rule will be left unstated, in which case the conclusion follows by analogy.

argument by analogy, a way not of proving things but of seeing things. And it is fundamental to what both Plato and Socrates understood by dialectic.

Socrates next turns to direct examination of the definition. Euthyphro has been brought to recognize that loving is prior to being loved, and now understands Socrates' question well enough to answer it: the holy is loved by the gods because it is holy, not holy because it is loved. With this admission, his definition collapses.

d   S. Then what are we to say about the holy, Euthyphro? Is it loved by all the gods, as your account has it?

     E. Yes.

     S. Because it is holy? Or for some other reason?

     E. No, for that reason.

     S. Then it is loved because it is holy, not holy because it is loved?

     E. It seems so.

     S. Moreover, what is loved and dear to the gods is loved because of their loving.

     E. Of course.

     S. Then what is dear to the gods is not (the same as) holy, Euthyphro, nor is the holy (the same as) dear to the gods, as you claim: the two are different.[1]

e   E. But why, Socrates?

     S. Because we agreed that the holy is loved because it is holy, not holy because it is loved.

     E. Yes.

     S. But what is dear to the gods is, because it is loved by the gods, dear to the gods by reason of this same loving; it is not loved because it is dear to the gods.

     E. True.

     S. But if in fact what is dear to the gods and the holy were the same, my friend, then, if the holy were loved because it is holy, what is dear to the gods would be

11a   loved because it is dear to the gods; but if what is dear to the gods were dear to the gods because the gods love it, the holy would be holy because it is loved. But as it is, you see, the opposite is true, and the two are completely different. For the one (what is dear to the gods) is of the sort to be loved

---

[1] οὐκ ἄρα τὸ θεοφιλὲς ὅσιον ἐστιν . . . οὐδὲ τὸ ὅσιον θεοφιλές, . . . ἀλλ' ἕτερον τοῦτο τούτου. See below, 15b–c.

because it is loved; the other (the holy), because it is of the sort to be loved, *therefore* is loved. It would seem, Euthyphro, that when you were asked what the holy is, you did not mean to make its nature and reality (οὐσία) clear to me; you mentioned a mere affection (πάθος) of it – the holy has been so affected as to be loved by all the gods. But what it really is, you have not yet said.

b

This concludes Socrates' examination of the second definition. The argument is one of some elegance.

Assume that what is dear to the gods and the holy are the same. Then (i) if the holy is loved because it is holy, what is dear to the gods is loved because it is dear to the gods. Consequent follows from antecedent by substitution.[1] But it has been agreed that the consequent is false (10c). Therefore, either the antecedent is false or the substitution impossible. But it has been agreed that the antecedent is true (10d). Therefore, the substitution is impossible: what is dear to the gods and the holy are not the same. Again, (ii) if what is dear to the gods is dear to the gods because they love it, the holy is holy because it is loved. Once more, consequent follows from antecedent by substitution. But it has been agreed that the consequent is false (10d). Therefore, either the antecedent is false or the substitution impossible. But it has been agreed that the antecedent is true (10c). Therefore, the substitution is impossible: what is dear to the gods and the holy are not the same.

In short, Euthyphro's definition implies an equivalence. But if either side of that equivalence is true, the other side is false. Thus the equivalence, and both of its component implications, are false. The definition must be rejected.

The strategy with which Socrates has conducted this argument deserves comment. When Euthyphro expresses confidence that the holy is what all the gods love, Socrates remarks, 'Perhaps, my friend, we shall learn better' (10a). He immediately goes on to ask whether the holy is loved because it is holy, or holy because it is loved, a question which proves crucial to the examination. In short, he knows from the beginning that the definition will not

---

[1] The basis for this substitution is, of course, intentional, in the sense that being loved by all the gods is supposed to *define* holiness, to say what it is. To construe the substitution extensionally, as a mere case of substitutibility *salva veritate*, is to miss the point of the argument. See P. T. Geach, *op. cit.*, pp. 376–7.

do, knows where the difficulty lies, and how to expose it. But he proceeds by indirection, establishing first a premise which seems irrelevant, the priority of loving to being loved; then, suddenly, he combines it with another premise, that the holy is loved by the gods because it is holy, and the definition is disproved. The whole procedure resembles nothing so much as a chess-player using an apparent diversion on the other side of the board to set up a combination, and then calling 'Checkmate'.

But what, after all, does the argument prove? Euthyphro made the mistake of supposing both that the holy is what all the gods love, and that they love it because it is holy. The result is a vicious circle, which Socrates has exposed with considerable ingenuity. But ingenuity is not instruction. A vicious circle is vicious because of incompatible premises, but to show their incompatibility is not to show which of them is false. The argument is supposed to prove that the holy cannot be defined as what all the gods love. It might as easily have been supposed to prove that the gods do not love the holy because it is holy.

The point, after all, is one of some importance. Euthyphro's definition is a motif in a persistent and recurring theme in European religious thought, the theme of theological voluntarism, the view that whatever is good is good because God wills it, that not even He is aware of a character of goodness distinct from His own will. This has its corollary in subjectivist theories of ethics which define goodness in terms of approval or favouring, attitudes which are supposed not to rest on awareness of any intrinsic value in objects. The similarity between the theological and ethical views is clear: a Platonist might say that their difference consists mainly in the difference between human ignorance and divine ignorance.

This begs the question. No voluntarist or subjectivist who knew what he was about would agree, as Euthyphro agrees, that approval may be evoked by recognition of a character in things which makes them intrinsically worthy of approval. Euthyphro's assumption that the holy is loved by the gods because it is holy betrays a mistaken understanding of his own position.

It is, in fact, odd that Euthyphro should have made that mistake. When first asked whether the holy is loved because it is holy, or holy because it is loved, he did not understand the question (10a). He was able to answer it only after Socrates provided examples of the distinction between activities and counterpart properties, and then, surprisingly, he answered it in a way clean counter to what one would expect. His definition makes the holy a mere special case of what is loved: it is what is loved by all the gods. Thus if loving is prior to being loved, it follows that the holy is holy because it is loved, not loved because it is holy. Euthyphro reverses this, with disastrous effect for his definition.

The reason, of course, is that the pull of common sense is strong. Euthyphro has already granted without question that the gods love what they believe beautiful, good, and just, and hate what they think the opposite (7e); the goodness in things is for him, as for most plain men, a reason for loving and not a consequence of it.[1] That is why, once the difference between loving and being loved is made clear, he so readily agrees that the gods love the holy because it is holy. But if Euthyphro's answer is dictated by common sense, it is also required by the assumption on which the discussion, so far as Socrates at least is concerned, proceeds: that holiness is a Form.

Within the framework of the discussion, then, Socrates' criticism of Euthyphro is quite justified: being loved by all the gods is not the nature and reality of the holy, its οὐσία, but only an affection of it, a fact about it, something which happens to be true of it, πάθος τι. If the holy is loved because it is holy, it cannot be defined, though it can perhaps be characterized, as something loved.

6. SECOND INTERLUDE: SOCRATES A DAEDALUS (11B–D)

Socrates now repeats his question: Just what is holiness? And Euthyphro, provoked and harassed, complains because he cannot say what he means. Socrates is a Daedalus, who makes arguments move around and refuse to stay put.

The complaint is a familiar one. Laches knows what he means by courage, and when Socrates cross-questions him, he is angry at himself because the words for it give him the slip (*Laches*, 194b). Polus is 'bound and gagged' by Socrates in an argument (*Gorgias*, 482e). Meno, his definition of virtue refuted, compares Socrates to a torpedo or electric ray, numbing anyone he touches (*Meno*, 80a).

---

[1] Cf. *Charmides*, 167e, *Lysis*, 218d–219a.

Daedalus, more famous for Icarian experiments in aviation, made statues so life-like they moved.

b   (*Socrates continues*) If you please, Euthyphro, do not conceal things from me: start again from the beginning and tell me what sort of thing the holy is. We will not quarrel over whether it is loved by the gods, or whether it is affected in other ways. But tell me in earnest: What is the holy and unholy?

E.   But, Socrates, I do not know how to tell you what I mean. Somehow everything I propose goes around in circles on us and will not stand still.

S.   Your words are like the works of my ancestor,
c   Daedalus.[1] If I had offered them, if I had put them forward, you would perhaps have laughed at me because my kinship to him makes my words run away and refuse to stay put. But as it is, you put them forward, and we must find another joke; it is for you that they refuse to stay, as you agree yourself.

E.   But, Socrates, the joke, I think, still tells. It is not me who makes them move around and not stay put. I
d   think you are the Daedalus. If it had been up to me, they would have stayed where they were.

S.   Then apparently, my friend, I am even more skilful than my venerated ancestor, inasmuch as he made only his own work move, whereas I make mine move and other people's too. And certainly the most subtle feature of my art is that I am skilled against my will. For I want arguments to stand still, to stand fixed and immovable. I want that more than
e   the wealth of Tantalus and the skill of Daedalus combined.

Socrates would rather see an argument stand fast than have legendary skill combined with legendary wealth. The moral seriousness of the man peeps out from behind the mask of ironical detachment.

Meno called Socrates a torpedo, because he numbed. But Socrates called himself a gadfly, sent by the god to sting the soul of Athens. He was to say at his trial (*Apology*, 30a–b):

I do nothing but go about persuading you all, young and old alike, not to care more about your persons or your property, but first and

[1] Cf. *Alcibiades*, I, 121a.

beyond all else to care about your soul, so that it may be as good as possible.

If there were those who doubted that he was in earnest, his death instructed them.

Yet his method of persuasion to moral excellence was peculiar. That method was *elenchus*, refutation, and at his trial he cited it as one of the chief reasons for the prejudice against him (*Apology*, 21c). To an observer, *elenchus* would have appeared perhaps equal parts banter and hair-splitting. To a respondent, perhaps a self-important politician cornered in the Agora, it must have seemed mainly to consist in subtle and unanswerable insult. This impression would not have been allayed by the behaviour of the crowd of young companions who followed Socrates about to see the sport, and imitated his example by using *elenchus* on other folk themselves. As Socrates remarked in the *Apology* (33c), 'It was not unamusing', and the humour of it all was a principal reason why he was indicted for corrupting the youth.

Elenchus looks like eristic. If Socrates' declared purpose in arguing was moral improvement, his apparent purpose seemed only to win.[1] And win he did, with impressive regularity. Even intelligent men trained in the arts of debate, such as Protagoras and Gorgias, could not make head against him. Dialectic so pursued seemed less like a form of inquiry or moral exhortation than a game, and this impression was not relieved by the fact that its results were ostensibly so negative: the early dialogues, where Plato's portrait of Socrates seems most consciously accurate, consistently end in failure.

But this is just the point. If Euthyphro, at the end of this dialogue, is still unable to say what holiness is, he will at least have better understood the question and its implications for his life; and he will have begun to understand that he does not know what he thought he knew. In the *Meno* (84a–b) Socrates claims that to learn that one is ignorant is a thing of great importance, and one of the greatest benefits which dialectic has to confer: for unless one realizes one's ignorance, one will have no motive to inquire.[2]

This, indeed, was the central point of Socrates' moral mission.

---

[1] A purpose he explicitly disclaimed. Thus he remarks to Critias (*Charmides*, 166d; cf. *Protagoras*, 348c–d), that it makes not a whit of difference whether it is Critias or Socrates who is refuted: the only important thing is the argument itself.

[2] Cf. *Symposium*, 204a.

The Apollo at Delphi had said that he was the wisest man in Greece, and in service to the god he set himself to test (not, as some translations have it, to refute) the meaning of the oracle. He found that his wisdom exceeded that of other men only in that he knew that he did not know, whereas they thought they knew and did not. So it is that Euthyphro thinks he knows what holiness is, and does not, and Socrates goes to school to him to refute him. His moral mission was examination: 'The unexamined life is not worth living' (*Apology*, 38a).

Back of this was the conviction that rational reflection on moral principle, prompted by awareness of one's own ignorance, is of the utmost importance in the living of a human life. The principles Socrates sought were Forms, standards fixed in the nature of things which would enable a man infallibly to judge the difference between right and wrong. Without knowledge of those principles, the moral life became guess-work, and guess-work marred by mistake.

Supreme confidence in the objectivity of moral principles, combined with doubt as to anyone's claim to understand their nature is a customary mark of the early dialogues. 'Human wisdom is a thing of little worth or none at all' (*Apology*, 23a). And yet, 'There is no evil that can come to a good man in life or in death, and the gods do not neglect his affairs' (*Apology*, 41d). A peculiar combination of scepticism and belief, and one which has marked many rationalists since his time – though rarely with such effect.

7. REQUIREMENTS FOR DEFINITION (11E–12A)

Socrates now undertakes to help Euthyphro along by asking whether the holy is part of the just. This question may be paraphrased, not inaccurately, as the question whether holiness is not a species of which justice is the genus. But it is well to remember that, though 'part' and 'whole', μέρος or μόριον and ὅλον, became ordinary philosophical Greek for 'species' and 'genus', Socrates' language is very concrete. In the *Protagoras* (329d; cf. 349b–c), when it is agreed that justice, temperance and holiness are parts of virtue, which is a single thing, Socrates asks whether they are parts as eyes, ears and nose are parts of the face, or parts like the parts of gold, which differ from each other only in size. And Protagoras thinks they are parts like the parts of the face.

(Socrates continues) But enough of this. Since you seem to be lazy and soft, I will come to your aid and help you teach me about the holy. Don't give up: ask yourself if you do not think that all the holy is necessarily just.

E. I do.

S. Then is all the just holy? Or is all the holy just, but not all the just holy – part of it holy, part something else?

E. I don't follow you, Socrates.

S. And yet you are as much wiser than I am as you are younger; as I said, you are lazy and soft because of your wealth of wisdom. My friend, extend yourself: what I mean is not hard to understand. I mean exactly the opposite of what the poet meant when he said that he was 'Unwilling to insult Zeus, the Creator, who made all things: for where there is fear there is also reverence'.[1] I disagree with him. Shall I tell you why?

E. Yes; certainly.

S. I do not think that 'where there is fear there is also reverence'. I think people fear disease and poverty and other such things – fear them, but have no reverence for what they fear. Do you agree?

E. Yes; certainly.

S. Where there is reverence, however, there is also fear. For if anyone stands in reverence and awe of something, does he not at the same time fear and dread the imputation of wickedness?[2]

E. Yes; he does.

S. Then it is not true that 'where there is fear there is also reverence'. But where there is reverence there is also fear, even though reverence is not in every place that fear is; fear is broader than reverence. Reverence is a part of fear just as odd is a part of number, and where there is number there is not also odd, but where there is odd there is also number. I imagine you follow me?

E. Yes; I do.

S. Well then, that is the sort of thing I had in mind when I asked if, where there is just, there is also holy. Or

12a

b

c

d

---

[1] *Stasinus*, Fr. 20 (Kinkel).
[2] Cf. *Crito*, 47d.

> is it rather that where there is holy there is also just,
> but holy is not in every place that just is, the
> holy being a part of the just. Shall we say that, or
> do you think differently?

E.   No. I think you are right.

S.   Then consider the next point. If the holy is part of the
just, it would seem that we must find out what
part of the just the holy is. Now, to take an example
we used a moment ago, if you were to ask me what
part of number the even is, and what kind of
number it is, I would say that it is number with
equal rather than unequal sides.[1] Do you agree?

E.   Yes; I do.

e   S.   Then try in the same way to teach me what part of the
just is holy, so that I may tell Meletus to wrong me
no longer, and not to indict me for impiety, since
I have already learned from you what things are
pious and holy and what are not.

If the holy is part of the just, it should be possible to specify what
part, as the even is that part of number divisible by two. Definition
proceeds by citing a genus common to many species, and a

---

[1] Literally, 'number which is not scalene but isosceles'. An Arethan scholium on
the Bodleian manuscript (see Burnet, *Euthyphro, ad loc.*) suggests that even numbers
are 'isosceles' because triangles with equal legs are bisectable, equally divisible into
two; this fits Plato's own definition of even number in the Laws (X, 895e). But it
seems odd to call a number scalene or isosceles (cf. Heath, *History of Greek Mathematics*, vol. i., p. 292), and it has been thought that Plato is here referring to some form
of geometrical representation of number. M. de Strÿcker (*Rev. des Étud. Grec.*, 1950,
pp. 44–49) suggests that the reference is to the familiar Pythagorean device of
representing number by gnomons (for which see Kirk and Raven, *The Presocratic
Philosophers*, pp. 243–55). He neglects, however, the decisive objection to this view:
gnomon representation makes odd numbers isosceles, since the ratio of their sides
is always one to one, and even numbers scalene, since their ratio is always different
for each number (cf. Aristotle, *Phys.* III 203a 10–15). This is precisely the reverse of
what is required; nor is there any other geometrical representation which fits the
passage.

The terms 'isosceles' and 'scalene' are in fact simply metaphors, whose explanation
has been kindly suggested to me by Professor Cherniss. ἰσοσκελής means equal-
legged; σκαληνός means uneven, unequal, or rough, and is probably related to
σκολιός crooked, bent, or twisted. Even numbers, being divisible into two equal and
integral parts, are 'isosceles'; odd numbers are scalene because they are not so
divisible – they limp.

difference which marks off the species under examination from all others.[1]

Socrates offers examples to help explain the relation of species to genus, part to whole.[2] One of them is arithmetical: the relation of odd to number. The other is psychological or religious: the relation of reverence to fear. Reverence is a part of fear, and narrower than fear: it is fear of the imputation of wickedness.[3] Also, even is a part of number: it is number which is not scalene, but isosceles – that is, number divisible by two. If the holy is part of the just, it should be possible to provide a similar account, to specify a difference which will make clear what part it is.

This account of Socrates' intention should be contrasted with another. Some students have found in this passage, not the lesson that species are to be distinguished from genera, but the lesson that *A* propositions – propositions which are both universal and affirmative – cannot be converted *simpliciter*. Thus, for example, the proposition that all whales are mammals does not imply that all mammals are whales, and in general 'All S is P' does not imply 'All P is S'.[4] It has been claimed that Socrates' suggestion that holiness, reverence, and odd, respectively, are parts of but narrower than justice, fear, and number, implies an explicit recognition of this rule.[5] In a similar way, it has been supposed that because, in the *Phaedo*, Socrates is made to reason syllogistically, Plato discovered the syllogism.

In estimating the force of this claim, it is well to bear in mind C. S. Peirce's distinction between *logica utens* and *logica docens*, logic as used and the science of logic. All of us, every day, use logic, use such principles as contradiction and excluded middle, *modus ponens* and *tollens*, categorical, hypothetical and disjunctive syllogism. If we did not, we should be unable to distinguish between

---

[1] Cf. *Definitions,* 414d.

[2] The term 'whole' is not used in this passage, but may be inferred from the use of 'part'. See περὶ ὅλης ἀρετῆς, *Laches,* 190c.

[3] Reverence and fear are treated, however, as distinct and co-ordinate at *Republic,* V, 465a.

[4] Though, of course, when S and P are chosen with specific meanings the conversion may hold, as in 'All Greeks are Hellenes'; but it then holds in virtue of its content, not its form.

[5] See also Protagoras' claim that, if all courageous men are bold, it does not follow that all bold men are courageous, *Protagoras,* 350c–d.

truth and falsehood, or make decisions, or fashion means to ends. But to say that these principles are used is not to say that, in their use, they are explicitly recognized: the average man is quite capable of rejecting a given specimen of reasoning as invalid without being able to say that all specimens of the same logical form are invalid, or why they are invalid, or, for that matter, what he means by invalidity. Those are questions for *logica docens*. It is just this distinction between *logica docens* and *logica utens* which explains the truth behind Locke's jibe that God was not so sparing to men as to make them barely two-legged, leaving it to Aristotle to make them rational. God was indeed not so sparing as so.

The question of whether Socrates is here attempting to establish that *A* propositions are not simply convertible reduces to the question of whether he is attempting to establish that propositions of a given logical form – namely, those which are universal and affirmative – are not subject to the logical operation of simple conversion. It was Aristotle who first stated this rule explicitly.[1] Was he then merely repeating a point made by the Platonic Socrates in the *Euthyphro*? Surely not. There is nothing in the early dialogues to suggest that propositions should be distinguished according to their logical form, or classified by quantity and quality – nor any hint of the Square of Opposition which such classification immediately suggests. More generally, there is no evidence in any Platonic dialogue, early or late, that Plato had any notion of logical form, any notion that relations might obtain between propositions simply in virtue of their structure rather than in virtue of the meaning of their terms. In this matter, Aristotle thought himself a pioneer, and Aristotle was right.[2] Socrates' concern in the *Euthyphro* is not with the logical form of propositions, but with relations holding between certain kinds of terms. If we are to apply the method of Example to his examples, the particular relation he has in view is the relation holding between terms which stand to each other as part to whole, as species to genus.

Each of Euthyphro's previous attempts at definition suffered from the same defect. They identified the holy with the things which have it, and undertook to mark off those things by a

---

[1] *Prior Analytics*, I, 25a, 5–25; note the qualification to the rule required by Aristotle's theory of the Predicables, *Topics*, II, 109a, 10–25.

[2] See F. M. Cornford, *Plato's Theory of Knowledge*, pp. 264–8, 276–7.

defining property: being loved by the gods, or being loved by all the gods. In view of the fact that 'the holy' could commonly mean things said to be holy, Euthyphro's mistake was a natural one. But a mistake it is. Socrates had asked to be told the nature of a Form of holiness, a universal which is the same in all holy things, a standard for determining what things are holy and what are not, an essence by which holy things are holy. But if the holy is identified with the things which have it, it can be none of these. It makes no sense to say that holy things are the same in all holy things, or that holy things are a standard for determining what things are holy and what things are not, or that holy things are that by which holy things are holy. Furthermore, Socrates has shown that a distinguishing mark of holy things is not necessarily the same as the holy: even if it were true that all those and only those things are holy which are loved by all the gods, this would still not express the essential nature of holiness. An extensional equivalence is not the same as an intensional equivalence: to borrow an example from Professor Quine, if all those and only those creatures with a heart are creatures with a kidney, it does not follow and is in fact false to suppose that 'creature with a kidney' is equivalent in sense to, or defines, 'creature with a heart'.

The association of holiness with justice is common throughout the dialogues,[1] but the precise status of holiness is far from clear. In the *Laches* (199d), *Meno* (78e) and *Protagoras* (330b; cf. 325a, 329c, 349b), it is treated as a companion-virtue to courage, temperance, justice, and wisdom, and not as a species of any of them. Had the dialectic of the *Euthyphro* continued in the direction it here begins to take, the proximate genus of holiness might have been identified as virtue, not as justice. On the other hand, holiness as a virtue does not play a prominent role in the middle and later dialogues. The *Republic* lists only four virtues as pimary: courage, justice, temperance, and wisdom – the Cardinal Virtues, as they came to be called. Precisely those virtues are listed in the *Laws* (631c–d) as divine goods, in contrast to such human goods as health, wealth, good looks, and strength. This suggests that Plato came to suppose that holiness, in terms of the internal order of the soul, represents nothing not already fully represented by the other

---

[1] Cf. *Crito*, 54b, *Republic*, II, 368b, X, 615b, *Theaetetus*, 176b, *Politicus*, 301d, *Laws*, II, 663b, d, XII, 959b. This list is representative, not exhaustive. See also Bluck, *Plato's* Meno, pp. 235, 262, and Adam, *op. cit.*, pp. xxxii ff.

virtues, and especially, perhaps, by justice.[1] The *Gorgias* (507a–b) follows the *Euthyphro* in maintaining that the sensible man (ὁ σώφρων) will do what is fitting both with respect to men and with respect to gods, and that doing what is fitting with respect to men is justice, while doing what is fitting with respect to gods is holiness. But when the locus of the virtues is once shifted from action and external behaviour, and placed rather in the inward parts of the soul, this distinction vanishes.[2]

Socrates' requirement that definition specify a genus marks an important advance in the dialectic of the *Euthyphro*. And it brings into sharp relief the fact that the object of definition is a Form, not the things which have it.

The dialectic of the *Euthyphro* here reaches a level at which other dialogues sometimes begin. In the *Protagoras* (329c) it is assumed early on that justice, temperance, and holiness are parts of virtue. Again, the dialectic of the *Laches* begins (190c–d) with the assumption that courage is a part of virtue, and the discussion aims, unsuccessfully, at finding a difference, finding out what part it is. On the other hand, the dialectic of the *Charmides*, *Lysis*, and *Hippias Major* never reaches this point at all, never gets beyond the level of abstraction represented by Euthyphro's first and second definitions – and Hippias, indeed, manages even that only with great difficulty.

8. THIRD DEFINITION: THE HOLY, MINISTRY TO THE GODS (12e–14b)

Following the analogy of number, Euthyphro now divides the just into two parts, that concerned with ministry to the gods, and that concerned with ministry to men. That part of the just concerned with ministry to the gods is the holy.[3]

The word here translated 'ministry' is θεραπεία, which corresponds closely in sense to the English word 'service'. The argument which follows is another example of Example:

---

[1] Professor Dodds (*Gorgias*, p. 336) suggests that the omission of holiness from the list of virtues in *Republic*, IV, 'may be due merely to the difficulty of fitting it into the scheme of virtues in relation to social classes'. But it is unlikely that Plato was compelled to leave it out because he could not find a way to put it in.

[2] See *Republic*, IV, 443c–d.

[3] Cf. *Gorgias*, 507a–b. The *Definitions* (412e–413a) define piety as 'Justice with respect to the gods; power of voluntary service to gods; right estimate of honour and worship due gods; knowledge of the honour and worship due gods'.

E. Well, Socrates, I think that that part of the just which is pious and holy is concerned with ministering to the gods, and the remaining part of the just is concerned with ministering to men.

S. Excellently put, Euthyphro. But there is still one small
    point left: I do not yet understand what you mean by 'ministering'. You surely do not mean that ministering to the gods is like ministering to other things, though I suppose we do talk that way, as when we say that it is not everyone who knows how to minister to horses, but only the horse-trainer. That is true, is it not?

E. Yes; certainly.

S. Because horse-training takes care of horses.

E. Yes.

S. And it is not everyone who knows how to minister to dogs, but only the huntsman.

E. True.

S. Because huntsmanship takes care of dogs.

b E. Yes.

S. And the same is true of herdsmanship and cattle?

E. Yes; certainly.

S. And holiness and piety minister to the gods, Euthyphro? Is that what you are saying?

E. Yes; it is.

S. Now, is not all ministering meant to accomplish the same thing? I mean this: to take care of a thing is to aim at some good, some benefit, for the thing cared for, as you see horses benefited and improved when ministered to by horse-training. Or do you not agree?

E. Yes; I do.

S. And dogs are benefited by huntsmanship, and cattle by
c herdsmanship, and similarly with other things as well – or do you think ministering can work harm to what is cared for?

E. No, by Zeus; not I.

S. But must be beneficial?

E. Of course.

S. Now, does holiness, which is to be a kind of ministering, benefit the gods? Does it improve them? Would you agree that when you do something holy you are making some god better?

E. No, by Zeus; not I.

> S. I did not think you meant that, Euthyphro. Far from it.
> d   That is why I asked you what you meant by mini-
>   stering to the gods: I did not believe you meant
>   such a thing as that.
> E. Yes; and you were right, Socrates. I did not mean that.

This is the first horn of a disguised dilemma. Holiness is service or ministry to the gods. But what does this mean? If A serves B, B may be the object of the service in the way that horses are the object of horse-training, or patients the object of physicians. To serve a thing in this sense is to aim at its benefit or improvement; but Euthyphro can hardly agree that holiness improves gods and makes them better.

On the other hand, A may serve B as servants commonly serve their masters, by helping them accomplish some further result at which they aim. An example of this sort of service is the service rendered to an artist, not as a man, but as an artist. To serve a physician *as* a physician is to help him produce or preserve health; to serve a ship-builder *as* a ship-builder is to help him produce a ship; to serve a house-builder *as* a house-builder is to help him produce a house. Euthyphro will find this alternative more con-genial: after all, the gods produce many noble products. Un-fortunately, he finds it impossible to say what product it is that they produce with our co-operation; how it is we serve their noble purposes. Holiness, then, is still left undefined, since no satis-factory meaning can be assigned to θεραπεία.

Plato marks the transition between the horns of this dilemma by a shift in vocabulary: θεραπεία, 'ministry', is replaced by the nearly synonymous ὑπηρετική, 'service'.

> S. Very well. But what kind of ministering to the gods is
>   holiness?
> E. The kind, Socrates, with which slaves minister to their
>   masters.
> S. I see. Holiness would, it seems, be a kind of service to
>   gods.
> E. Quite so.
> S. Now, can you tell me what sort of product service to
>   physicians would be likely to produce? Would it
>   not be health?
> E. Yes.
> e S. What about service to ship-builders? Is there not some
>   product it produces?

E. Clearly it produces a ship, Socrates.

S. And service to house-builders produces a house?

E. Yes.

S. Then tell me, my friend: What sort of product would service to gods produce? Clearly you know, for you say you know better than anyone else about religious matters.

E. Yes; and I am telling the truth, Socrates.

S. Then in the name of Zeus, tell me: What is that fine product which the gods produce by using us as servants?

E. They produce many things, Socrates, excellent things.

14a *S.* So do generals, my friend, but still their work can be summed up quite easily. Generals produce victory in war. Not so?

E. Of course.

S. And farmers produce many excellent things, but still their work can be summed up as producing food from the earth.

E. Yes; of course.

S. But what about the many excellent things the gods produce? How does one sum up their production?

b *E.* I told you a moment ago, Socrates, that it is difficult to learn accurately how things stand in these matters. Speaking freely, however, I can tell you that if a man knows how to say and do things acceptable to the gods in prayer and sacrifice, those things are holy; and they preserve both families and cities and keep them safe. The opposite of what is acceptable to the gods is impious, and impiety overturns and destroys all things.

S. You could have summed up the answer to my question much more briefly, Euthyphro, if you had wished. But you are not eager to instruct me; I see that c now. In fact, you just came right up to the point and turned away, and if you had given me an answer, I would already have learned holiness from you. But as it is, the questioner must follow the answerer wherever he leads.[1]

---

[1] Reading τὸν ἐρωτῶντα τῷ ἐρωτωμένῳ, an emendation suggested by T.W. Burnet, following Bt, read τὸν ἐρῶντα τῷ ἐρωμένῳ, 'the lover must follow the loved one'. But this gives an inferior sense, and Burnet's claim *ad loc.* that it is the answerer who must follow the questioner in dialectic, however true that may be in (say)

It is sometimes supposed that the *Euthyphro* is a masked dialogue, the failure at its conclusion only ostensible. It is supposed that Socrates' own definition of the holy is adumbrated here: it is the co-operation of men with gods in effecting excellent or noble products.[1]

The flaw in this assumption is that, if holiness is a virtue, a species of justice, it has no product. When Polemarchus in the *Republic* (I, 332c ff.) defines justice as the art of benefiting friends and harming enemies, Socrates is quick to put him right: it is the doctor who can do this best in time of sickness, the general in time of war. If you wish to benefit or harm a person, it is some specific art or skill which will show you how. If usefulness is to be defined in terms of a concrete product, an ἔργον, such as health or victory in war or food from the fields, then virtue is useless.[2] It is no accident that Euthyphro cannot name a product which holiness produces. It could have a product only if it were not a virtue.

9. FOURTH DEFINITION: THE HOLY, AN ART OF PRAYER AND SACRIFICE (14C–15C)

Following Euthyphro's own suggestion (14b), Socrates now leads him to say that holiness is knowledge of how to pray and sacrifice.

The word translated 'knowledge', ἐπιστήμη, is often equivalent to τέχνη, 'art', and is so used here. This definition differs from the previous one in that the holy is to be a species of art, not of justice; the question of whether justice may not itself be a species of art is left undiscussed.

Prayer and sacrifice require art because they involve, not merely giving to the gods and receiving from them, but also, as Socrates points out, *right* giving and *right* receiving. Sacrifices may be unacceptably performed; ritual, after all, proceeds by rule, and if

---

[1] See above, pp. 6–7. The textual support for this has been found in Socrates' remark to Euthyphro at 14c: 'You just came right up to the point and turned away.' But this, in context, suggests only that the 'What is it?' question can be answered, not that Euthyphro has succeeded in answering it.

[2] Cf. *Charmides*, 165e, 162e, *Republic*, I, 346a, *Gorgias*, 452e.

---

the *Parmenides* or *Sophist*, is refuted for the early dialogues by *Meno*, 75d. Burnet cites Schanz for ἐρωτωμένῳ; but it was read by Bekker in 1826, and is almost certainly far older: Ficino translated, '*necesse est enim interrogantem interrogatum sequi quacunque ducit*'. See above, p. 2, and also W. A. Heidel, *Plato's* Euthyphro, pp. 101–2.

it does not produce the result intended, it is an easy inference that the rules were broken. Again, prayers may be misdirected, and misdirected prayers were sometimes answered: witness Theseus, who prayed when he cursed Hippolytus, his son, for an adultery he did not commit.[1] The elderly Athenian in the *Laws* remarks that the prayer of the fool is dangerous: if he were not wholly a fool, he would pray to be given the opposite of what he desires (III, 688c).

It is perhaps in keeping with this that the one prayer attributed to Socrates in the dialogues should be a prayer for personal goodness.[2] It is offered in a grove on the Ilissus outside the walls of Athens, a little way from the spot where Boreas carried off Oreithuia from the stream: 'O beloved Pan, and ye other gods, as many as are in this place, grant that I may become beautiful within; and let as many external things as I possess be at harmony with what is in me. Let me think the wise man rich; and let me have that wealth which only the temperate man may bear and carry.'[3]

> (*Socrates continues*) But again, what do you say the holy and holiness is? Is it not knowledge of how to pray and sacrifice?
>
> E. It is.
>
> S. Now to sacrifice is to give to the gods, and to pray is to ask something from them?
>
> E. Exactly, Socrates.
>
> d   S. Then by this account, holiness is knowledge of how to ask from and give to the gods.
>
> E. Excellent, Socrates. You have followed what I said.
>
> S. Yes, my friend, for I am enamoured of your wisdom and attend to it closely, so naturally what you say does not fall to the ground wasted. But tell me, what is the nature of this service we render the gods? You say it is to ask from them and give to them?
>
> E. Yes; I do.
>
> S. Now, to ask rightly is to ask for things we need from them?
>
> E. Certainly.

[1] See *Laws*, III, 687d–e, VII, 801b–c.
[2] There is one other prayer, by Timaeus at *Critias*, 106a–b.
[3] *Phaedrus*, 279b–c.

e S. And again, to give rightly is to give in return what they happen to need from us? For surely there would be no skill involved in giving things to someone that he did not need.

E. You are right, Socrates.

S. So the art of holiness would be a kind of business transaction between gods and men.

E. Yes; if it pleases you to call it that.

S. Why, nothing pleases me unless it happens to be true. But tell me, what benefit do the gods gain from the gifts they receive from us? It is clear to everyone what they give, for we have nothing good they have not given. But how are they benefited by what they get from us? Or do we claim the larger share in the transaction to such an extent that we get all good from them, and they nothing from us?

E. But, Socrates, do you think the gods benefit from the things they receive from us?

S. Why, Euthyphro, whatever would these gifts of ours to the gods then be?

E. What do you suppose, other then praise and honour and as I just said, things which are acceptable?[1]

b S. Then the holy is what is acceptable, Euthyphro, and not what is beneficial or loved by the gods?

E. I certainly think it is loved by the gods, beyond all other things.

S. Then, on the contrary, the holy is what is loved by the gods.[2]

E. Yes, that beyond anything.

S. Will it surprise you if, in saying this, your words get up and walk? You call me a Daedalus. You say I make them walk. But I say that you are a good deal more skilful than Daedalus, for you make them walk in circles. Or are you not aware that our account has gone round and come back again to

c the same place? Surely you remember that, in what went before, the holy proved not to be the same as what is loved by the gods; the two were different. Do you recall?

---

[1] The *Definitions*, which reflect the tradition of the Academy, define 'holy' as 'service to god which is pleasing to god' (415a). This definition, of unknown date, was plainly suggested by the third and fourth definitions of the *Euthyphro*.

[2] Note the ambiguity in *is* as between οὐσία and πάθος; cf. 10d.

1ṣa

E. Yes; I recall.

E. Then do you not now realize that you are saying that what is loved by the gods is holy? But that is in fact something other than dear to the gods, is it not?

E. Yes.

S. Then either we were wrong a moment ago in agreeing to that, or, if we were right in assuming it then, we are wrong now.

E. It seems so.

Euthyphro has agreed that if holiness is an art of prayer and sacrifice, it is an art of right asking and right giving. He has also agreed that right giving is giving what the gods have need of. Yet surely, if the gods need a thing, they must benefit from getting it, and Euthyphro denies that the gods benefit from our gifts. If this is true, there can be no right giving to the gods, and holiness, therefore, cannot be defined as an art of prayer and sacrifice. The fourth definition has been refuted.

It is at this point that Euthyphro suggests that our gifts to the gods are honour, praise, and things which are acceptable. He has divine warrant for the claim: 'Hector was dearest to the gods of all mortals that are in Ilios. So was he to me at least, for nowise failed he in the gifts I loved. Never did my altar lack seemly feast, drink-offering and the steam of sacrifice, even the honour that falleth to our due.'[1] But Socrates proceeds to extract from this a new definition: the holy is the acceptable. His procedure is something less than sympathetic, but it is justified: with the old definition gone, a new one is needed. He goes on to suggest that if holiness is what is acceptable, it is not what is loved by the gods, and at this point Euthyphro, caught off balance, and none too clear on the difference between definition and mere connection, between the ὀυσία of holiness and a πάθος of it, suffers relapse. The Daedalus of the argument has brought things back to where they began.

In discussing definition, Socrates had used the example of reverence and fear in explaining the relation between species and genus. Reverence is a part of fear, being fear of the imputation of wickedness (12b–c). This is the only point in the *Euthyphro* where the inner attitudes and feelings of the worshippers are mentioned,

---

[1] Zeus to Hera, *Iliad*, xxiv, 66, trans. Lang, Leaf, and Myers.

a fact which will seem strange to the modern reader, for whom this element of religion may well seem part of its essence; he will also miss any reference to creed or dogma. But traditional Greek religion was largely a matter of δρώμενα, things done, ritual observance; it was hardly at all a matter of how the worshipper felt in his observance, or what he thought it meant. Aristotle supposed it distinctive of the mystery religions that they aimed to put the worshipper in a certain state of mind and give him a certain sort of experience.[1] Traditional Greek religion was neither dogmatic nor mystical nor evangelical.

The lack of creed and dogma in Greek religious observance barred settled standards of orthodoxy in belief, and this fact bears on Socrates' indictment for impiety. At his trial, Socrates summarized the charges against him as 'corrupting the youth and not acknowledging (νομίζοντα) the gods which the City acknowledges, but acknowledging strange gods'.[2] The verb here translated 'acknowledge', νομίζειν, is connected with νομός, a noun which meant both custom and law; as Burnet points out *ad loc.*, the charge was one of nonconformity in religious practice, not of unorthodoxy in religious belief. A γραφὴ ἀσεβείας, or indictment for impiety, could be lodged only in cases of sacrilege or blasphemy affecting the worship of the State; Euthyphro reflects a generally held opinion when he says (14b) that proper observance 'preserves families and cities and keeps them safe', and it was out of concern for the City's safety that impiety was prosecuted through public indictment. Socrates was charged with impiety, as Anaxagoras had been before him, because his pursuit of philosophy was thought to undermine ancestral custom[3] – guilt, so to speak, by implication.

The implication was one of which Socrates, at least, was unaware. His religious attitudes and observance appear to have been both conventional and sincere; Xenophon, in his defence of Socrates, particularly stressed this point, and Plato exhibits it

[1] Frag. 15 (Rose).

[2] *Apology*, 24b. The exact terms of the indictment are probably given in *Diogenes Laertius*, II, 40; cf. Xenophon, *Memorabilia*, I, i, 1.

[3] This explains the connection of the charge of impiety with that of corrupting the youth. It also explains its connection with the charge of acknowledging strange gods; in Athens you could acknowledge what gods you pleased, so long as you continued to acknowledge the ones you began with, and did not so act or speak as to undermine their worship.

often without describing it. This, of course, was quite consistent with his customary claim that, in these and other matters, he knew only that he did not know. In this connection, it is interesting to consider Socrates' last words in the *Phaedo* (118a): 'Crito, we owe a cock to Asclepius; do not neglect to pay it.' The report is likely enough to be accurate. It has been claimed that Socrates thus intended a thank-offering to the god of healing for being cured of the disease of life. A pretty notion, and romantic, but, like many such notions, removed from fact. The 'we' is not editorial, but plural, and the debt, therefore, was one which Socrates and Crito shared in common; nor is there evidence, in the *Phaedo* or elsewhere, that life was to be regarded as a disease. The debt was mentioned because the debt was owed, and if a hidden meaning must be sought in this, it is that, dying on a charge of impiety, Socrates' final words were, not ironical, but constitutive of an irony.

10. CONCLUSION (15C–16A)

Four attempts to define holiness have failed, and Socrates, implacable, repeats his question. But Euthyphro has lost heart.

Proteus, the 'old man of the sea', was shepherd of the seals, and perhaps a seal himself. He knew the intentions of the gods and the fate of absent friends, and if one could capture him and hang on to him when he was caught, he would tell. But it was hard to hold him: '(He) will assume all manner of shapes of all things that move upon the earth, and of the water, and of wondrous blazing fire. Yet do ye hold him unflinchingly and grip him yet the more.'[1]

S. Let us begin again from the beginning, and ask what the holy is. For I shall not willingly give up until I
d   learn. Please do not scorn me: bend every effort of your mind and now tell me the truth. You know it if any man does, and, like Proteus, you must not be let go before you speak. For if you did not know the holy and the unholy with certainty, you could not possibly undertake to prosecute your aged father for murder in behalf of a hired man. You would fear to risk the gods, lest your action be wrongful; and you would be ashamed before men.

[1] *Odyssey*, IV, 417–19, trans. A. T. Murray. Plato uses this comparison several times when dialectic goes awry. See *Euthydemus*, 288b, and *Ion*, 541e.

e   But as it is, I am confident that you think you know with certainty what is holy and what is not. So say it, friend Euthyphro. Do not conceal what it is you believe.

E. Some other time, Socrates. Right now I must hurry somewhere and I am already late.

S. What are you doing, my friend! You leave me and cast me down from my high hope, that I should learn from you what things are holy and what are not, and escape the indictment of Meletus by showing

16a   him that, due to Euthyphro, I am now wise in religious matters, that I no longer ignorantly indulge in loose speech and innovation, and most especially, that I shall live better the rest of my life.

The dialogue here ends. If Euthyphro persisted in his suit, he did so on another day; he will not now wait to see the King.[1] His action, though not his words, indicates that he has begun to learn the lesson which Socrates' questioning was designed to teach: that he is ignorant of things in which he thought himself wise.

The dialogue ends, as the *Laches*, *Charmides*, and *Hippias Major* end, on a note of apparent failure. Socrates has not learned what holiness is, and Euthyphro cannot teach him. But the dialectic has brought out a number of things which Plato, in later life, thought both important and true. In the last of his works, the *Laws*, an elderly Athenian Stranger, surrogate for Plato himself, offers a 'prelude' to legislation which indicates where, had Euthyphro been a wiser man, with greater insight into the fundamental unity of virtue, the discussion might have tended:[2]

> What life is agreeable to God, and becoming in His followers? One only, expressed for all in the old saying that 'like agrees with like, measure with measure', but things which have no measure agree neither with themselves nor with the things which have. Now God ought to be to us the measure of all things, and not man, as men commonly say: the words are far more true of Him. And he who would be dear to God must, as far as possible, be like Him and such as He is. Wherefore the temperate man is the friend of God, for he is like Him; and the intemperate or

---

[1] Burnet (*Euthyphro*, p. 2) inferred from 15e that Euthyphro had already seen the King, and that his business was over for the day. But if that were true, the introduction to the dialogue would surely have suggested it, and it does not.

[2] *Laws*, IV, 716c–717a, trans. Jowett (4th ed.).

unjust man is unlike Him and different from Him. And the same applies to other things; and this is the conclusion, which is also the noblest and truest of sayings – that for the good man to offer sacrifice to the gods, and hold converse with them by means of prayers and offerings and every kind of service, is the noblest and best of all things, and also the most conducive to a happy life, and very fit and meet. But with the bad man, the opposite of this is true; for the bad man has an impure soul, whereas the good is pure; and from one who is polluted, neither a good man nor God can without impropriety receive gifts. Wherefore the unholy do only waste their much service upon the gods, but when offered by an holy man, such service is most acceptable to them. This is the mark at which we ought to aim.

Despite differences in feeling and tone of thought natural to widely separate traditions, Plato's final views on morality and religion had something in common with those of the author of the Twenty-fourth Psalm.

III

PLATO'S EARLIER THEORY
OF FORMS

INTRODUCTION

The *Euthyphro* ends in failure: no definition of holiness is stated, and none is implied. There is no 'mask' which can be stripped off the dialogue to reveal its true meaning; it bears its meaning on its face.

To say this is not to say that the dialogue has no determinate philosophical content. W. A. Heidel once remarked of the *Euthyphro* that 'None of the briefer Platonic dialogues can be compared with it for the value of its suggestions toward philosophical theory',[1] and this is surely true. The interest of the dialogue does not lie in the product of its dialectic, for there is no product; it lies in the dialectic itself. That dialectic proceeds on the basis of assumptions about the essence or nature of things which regulate its work; and if that work ends in failure, with no definition of holiness achieved, the touchstone of failure lies precisely in the rules which guided the search.

Those rules, and the assumptions on which they rest, constitute a (not *the*) theory of Forms. It is a theory which operates much more at the level of assumption than explicit statement, but a theory none the less, and one whose elements may be put with some precision. Socrates' aim in the *Euthyphro* is to obtain an answer to the question, 'What is holiness?' He assumes, in pursuing his inquiry, that there is an ἰδέα, or εἶδος, a Form, of holiness, and that this Form is a universal, the same in all holy things (5d, 6d–e). He further supposes that that Form may be used as a standard, by which to judge what things are holy and what are not (6e); that it is an essence, by which or in virtue of

---

[1] *Plato's Euthyphro*, p. 27.

which holy things are holy (6d); and that it is capable of real or essential definition (11a, 12c–d). These assumptions constitute a theory of Forms.

That theory is both logical and metaphysical. Logically, Forms play a regulative role in dialectic: as antecedents of 'it' in the question 'What is it?' they determine the kinds of answer which are acceptable, and more importantly, unacceptable, in Socrates' search for definition. They define the conditions for deciding when dialectic has succeeded, and when it has failed. Metaphysically, Forms affect the career of the world: they are the real natures of things, and the world is what it is because they are what they are.

These two sides of Plato's theory meet in the notion of real definition. Dialectic is governed by rule, and directed toward the nature of things. Its rules are determined by its aim. To say that Forms exist is to say that real definition should be pursued; to say that real definition should be pursued is to say that Forms exist. The theory of Forms in the *Euthyphro* is not a superstructure gracelessly added on to dialectic: it is the foundation of dialectic. Without it, dialectic would not proceed by the rules it uses, or work toward the goal at which it aims. Socratic moral inquiry is inquiry about reality.

For all its likenesses, the theory of Forms assumed in the *Euthyphro* is not to be identified with the theory found in Plato's middle dialogues. Burke once remarked that 'though no man can draw a stroke between the confines of night and day, yet light and darkness are upon the whole tolerably distinguishable'. It is so with the early and the middle dialogues. The difference between the *Euthyphro* on the one hand, and the *Phaedo* and *Republic* on the other, is perhaps not the difference of light and darkness. But it is tolerably plain. The philosophy of the middle dialogues is a nest of coupled contrasts: Being and Becoming, Appearance and Reality, Permanence and Flux, Reason and Sense, Body and Soul, Flesh and the Spirit. Those contrasts are rooted in an ontology of Two Worlds, separated by a gulf of deficiency. The World of Knowledge, whose contents are the eternal Forms, stands to the World of Opinion, whose contents are sensible and changing, as the more real stands to the less real, as originals stand to shadows and reflections. The visible world is an image, unknowable in its deficiency, of an intelligible world apprehended by reason alone. If the seeds of this view are sown in early dialogues such as the *Euthyphro*, they have not there yet been brought to harvest.

I. FORMS AS REGULATIVE PRINCIPLES OF DIALECTIC

The central question of the *Euthyphro*, 'What is holiness?' is phrased in a variety of ways.[1] In itself, it is inherently ambiguous: it does not prescribe whether an example, or a distinguishing mark, or an account of essence is required to answer it. But Socrates, in asking Euthyphro to explain the characteristic itself (αὐτὸ τὸ εἶδος) by which holy things are holy – that is, to explain τὴν ἰδέαν τίς ποτέ ἐστιν (6d–e), 'what this character is' – makes the question more precise.

Forms as Universals

In asking for the ἰδέα, or Form, of holiness, Socrates expects to be told what is the same (ταὐτόν, 5d) in every holy action. When Euthyphro replies with questionable examples of holiness, he is reminded that his examples are not exhaustive; other things are holy too, and what Socrates wants is the nature of the Form they all have (ἔχον, 5d).

This pattern of argument is found in other dialogues. In the *Laches* (191e–192b), when courage is defined by the example of courage in battle, Socrates argues that this is not enough. Courage is found, not only in war, but in perils at sea, disease, poverty, and politics, and what he wishes to be told is what is the same (ταὐτόν) in all these things. In the *Hippias Major* (300a–b), Socrates claims that if two different things are beautiful, they must have something identical (τι τὸ αὐτό) which makes them beautiful, and that this common thing (τὸ κοινὸν τοῦτο) must be present to them. When Meno, in an early middle dialogue, undertakes to define virtue by giving a list of examples, Socrates corrects him with an analogy. Suppose you are asked what a bee is. There are many different kinds of bees, but it does no good to name them; bees do not differ as bees, and the question demanded some account of the common character all bees share. So it is with virtue: 'However diverse and multitudinous the virtues may be,

---

[1] See 5c 9; 6d 2 and 11b 2; 5d 7; 9c 5; 11b 1; 15c 11. See also *Laches* 190b, d, e; *Charmides* 159a; *Hippias Major* 286d, e.

they have all a characteristic (εἶδος) which makes them to be virtues, and it is on this that anyone who would say what virtue is must fix his gaze' (*Meno*, 72c).

As universals, Forms play a regulative role in dialectic; they are the antecedents of ἐστί in questions of τί ἐστί, 'What is it?', and they therefore specify the nature of that question, and so restrict the range of answers which may sensibly be given to it. 'What is the holy?' or 'What is the beautiful?' simply in terms of grammatical form, could be a request for an example of holiness or beauty;[1] and both Euthyphro and Hippias initially interpret Socrates' question in just this way. Even the abstract noun, as contrasted with the neuter adjective and article, is open to this meaning: Charmides attempts to say what σωφροσύνη, temperance, is by giving an example of temperance. But Socrates, who is seeking for an ἰδέα or Form which is the same in all its instances, and something all instances have, rules this out; because holiness and temperance and beauty are universals, answers to the question of what they are cannot merely provide examples of them.

Forms as Standards

Socrates wishes to be told the nature of holiness in order to use it as a standard or model, by which to tell what things are holy and what are not. The Form of holiness will be fitted for this office by reason of the fact that holy things are of such sort as (τοιοῦτον) it (6e). Similarly, in the *Lysis*, hair white with age is of the same sort as (οἷον) whiteness – of the same sort as what is present to it (217c–d).

The words τοιοῦτος (*talis*) and οἷος (*qualis*) are respectively demonstrative and indefinite pronouns correlative with the interrogative ποῖος, 'Of what sort?' Their use suggests that there is some sort of resemblance between the instances of Forms and Forms, a suggestion supported by the fact that the Form is described as a standard or παράδειγμα. But this suggestion is hardly an implication. The use of οἷον at *Gorgias*, 460b, for example, involves, not resemblance, but what Aristotle was later to call paronymy.[2] In the *Protagoras*, its use involves either identity or

---

[1] Thus, for example, τί ἐστι τοῦτο τὸ καλόν at *Euthydemus* 273d means, 'What is this fine thing (that you teach)?'

[2] *Categories*, 1a, 12 ff.

mutual implication.[1] And at *Phaedrus*, 246a, it is contrasted with resemblance. The fact is that the use of these words is fluid, and becomes determinate only in specific contexts. τοιοῦτον need not imply resemblance at *Euthyphro*, 6e; and it is worth noting that though Plato had at his disposal a rich and varied vocabulary of resemblance, he nowhere in the early dialogues calls instances of Forms μιμήματα or εἰκόνες or ὁμοιώματα of Forms, or describes their relations to Forms with verbs derived from the roots of these nouns.[2]

The claim that instances of Forms resemble Forms is not, then, implied by the text of the *Euthyphro*. Furthermore, it is uneconomical, since the text may be understood without it.[3] The Form of holiness is to serve as a standard for distinguishing things which are holy from things which are not. But surely the reason it is fitted to perform this function is that it is the nature of holy things in so far as they are holy. It is for this reason that Socrates supposes that if it is once understood what holiness in itself is, that knowledge will enable the knower to distinguish things which are holy from things which are not. So holiness is a standard for detecting things which are of such sort as it – that is, things which are instances of it.

This interpretation fits its context. Epistemologically, Forms are standards for detecting their instances. The ontological ground for this function is that instances have the Form (5d), and that the Form is that by which its instances are what they are (6d).

It is important to realize that Socrates' assumption that Forms are standards is as directly embedded in his 'What is it?' question as the assumption that Forms are universals. The question, 'What

---

[1] 330a–b; cf. 331b.

[2] Valuable things are described as εἴδωλα of the Primary Valuable at *Lysis*, 219d, but the relation between instances of Forms is not, directly at least, there in view, but rather the relation of means to ends, and the use of this term does not in any case imply resemblance in any ordinary sense: medicine is an εἴδωλον of health, but does not, surely, *resemble* health.

[3] Depending on how resemblance is construed, it may also be illogical. If the resemblance of instances of holiness to holiness is taken to imply that holiness is itself an instance of holiness, then, since knowledge of the Form was sought to identify instances of holiness, reference to some further Form would be required to identify the Form. Cf. H. F. Cherniss, 'The Philosophical Economy of the Theory of Ideas', *SPM*, p. 3.

is the holy?' is prompted in the *Euthyphro* by a practical problem of identification: it is important to find out what holiness is in order to know what sorts of action are holy and what sorts are not. One cannot know whether a given action is holy without knowing what holiness is (6e, 9a–c, 15d–e), any more than one can be certain that two men are friends without knowing what friendship is (*Lysis*, 223b), or that a speech is beautiful without knowing what beauty is (*Hippias Major*, 286c–d). Knowing the Form is a condition for recognizing its instances: to ask what holiness is, is to ask for knowledge of a criterion by which to distinguish things which are holy from things which are not.

This demand for a criterion is essential to Socratic dialectic, which is directed, not merely toward abstract understanding, but toward the right ordering of life; the aim of dialectic is to understand the principles of that order, and to gain means to identify them in concrete instances. In the *Republic* (I, 344d–e) it is claimed that it is important to know what is holy and what is just and what is virtuous, because on that knowledge depends the conduct of a life. In the *Charmides* (175e), the young Charmides is said to be most temperate; but without knowing temperance, he will have no advantage from its presence in his life – this to a man who later became one of the Thirty Tyrants. If the aim of dialectic is to define a Form, the practical aim is the discernment of Form in things. 'Is not the holy itself in itself the same in every action? And the unholy in turn, the utter opposite of the holy, is it not the same as itself, and does not everything which is to be unholy possess one single characteristic with respect to unholiness?'[1]

Because Forms are universals common to many different instances, certain kinds of answer to the 'What is it?' question

---

[1] *Euthyphro*, 5d. Mr John Gould (*Plato's Ethics*) has said that, 'A . . . troublesome idea which we must abandon is the supposition that ἐπιστήμη, in Plato's writings, bases its claim to acknowledged supremacy in the sphere of ethics (and human behaviour in general) on being in direct touch with objective truths or objective values' (p. 11). And again, '. . . [The] fundamental factor in Socratic thinking was not, as some commentators have felt, intellectual, but a quality of faith, of faith in the ability of the individual to attain a "technique" of morality, and to achieve the practical assurance that the possession of a technical skill alone can give' (p. 66). But Mr Gould does not mention the passage quoted above, or other passages similar to it.

are ruled out: namely, all those answers which attempt to define by example – that is, by citing instances. Because Forms are standards, another sort of answer is ruled out: the sort of answer which would imply that holiness or temperance or beauty might in any way be unholy or intemperate or ugly. Forms are not qualified by their opposites.

It is on precisely this point that Socrates' examination of the first definition in the *Euthyphro* turns. Holiness can be unholy no more than jutice can be unjust.[1] Because this is so, and because what is loved by the gods is also hated by the gods and thus unholy, the holy cannot be what is loved by the gods. In the *Republic* it is a sufficient refutation of a proposed definition of justice, as telling the truth and paying one's debts, to point out that those actions may sometimes be just, but sometimes unjust; if a friend lent you weapons and then went mad, it would not be right to give them back when he asked for them; nor would one speak only the truth to a madman. So telling the truth and returning what one owes is not the definition of justice.[2]

There is an application of the principle that Forms cannot be qualified by their opposites in the *Hippias Major*. When Hippias undertakes to define beauty as a beautiful maiden, Socrates calls his attention to the fact that this is too narrow; there are beautiful mares and beautiful lyres and beautiful pots, besides beautiful maidens. Hippias objects to the pot. A worthless and trivial thing, he thinks, not at all beautiful in comparison to a mare or a maiden. Socrates replies that a pot, after all, may be beautiful in its kind, and that even a beautiful maiden may be ugly compared to a goddess. What, then, is beauty itself? That question cannot be answered by citing things which, in different comparisons, are no more beautiful than ugly. Hippias next suggests that the beautiful is gold; but when Socrates refutes this by showing circumstances in which gold, or the presence of gold, is not beautiful, Hippias begins to see the point: 'You seem to me to be seeking the reply that the beautiful must be

---

[1] Cf. *Protagoras*, 330c–e.

[2] *Republic*, I, 331b–d; cf. 339c–e. It should be noted that this passage may be interpreted as merely an example of the principle that a definition should not be too broad: the definition is not rejected on the ground that it implies that the same thing will be *both* just and unjust at once, which is the difficulty with Euthyphro's first definition of holiness.

something of such sort that it will never prove ugly to anyone anywhere.' To this Socrates replies, 'Quite right, Hippias. Now you understand me beautifully' (291d).

The principle that Forms are not qualified by their own opposite is directly connected with the self-identity of Forms. Socrates began the dialectic of the *Euthyphro* by suggesting that holiness is αὐτὸ αὐτῷ, the same by itself, and that its opposite, unholiness, is αὐτῷ ὅμοιον, like (or the same) as itself (5d). He is, then, seeking the nature of holiness *as such*. This suggestion is expanded at 7a to mean that holiness is not identical with unholiness, but its utter opposite,[1] and the refutation of Euthyphro's definition of holiness as what is loved by the gods is so stated as to imply that the definition violates this principle: you cannot say what holiness is by stating ὁ τυγχάνει ταὐτὸν ὂν ὅσιον τε καὶ ἀνόσιον, 'What same thing happens to be both holy and unholy', (8a). The assumption here is that if holiness were in any way unholy, it would not be the opposite of unholiness, and the intuitive principle underlying this inference is clear: that by which or in virtue of which things are holy is holiness as such, and cannot itself be unholy. The self-identity of Forms implies the radical exclusion of their opposites, and that exclusion is directly connected with the use of the Form as a standard. It can never be a true answer to the question, 'What is the holy?' to name something which is in any way unholy.

Forms as Essences

By Aristotle's account,[2] the essence of holiness would be that which holiness is καθ' αὐτό, in and of itself, or as such, and the account of which is a definition. This is precisely the force of

---

[1] Cf. *Protagoras* 330c: the claim that δικαιοσύνη, justice, is, or is οἷον, δίκαιον, just, and not ἄδικον, unjust, is an affirmation of the self-identity of justice, and therefore of its exclusion of its opposite, injustice. English is a more analytical language than Greek, not only in its grammatical, but in its logical syntax: 'Justice is just' cannot mean 'Justice is identical with justice'; but δικαιοσύνη δίκαιόν ἐστι can mean this, since δίκαιον (πρᾶγμα) may be used as an abstract noun, equivalent in meaning to δικαιοσύνη. For evidence that it is so used here, compare 330a–b with 331b. The claim that nothing else would be holy, εἰ μὴ αὐτή γε ἡ ὁσιότης ὅσιον ἔσται, 'unless holiness itself is holy' (330d–e), means that nothing would be holy if holiness were not the same as itself, and therefore radically exclusive of its opposite, unholiness. The point is that made in *Euthyphro*, 5d and 7a.

[2] Cf. *Metaphysics*, VII, iv.

74

Plato's formulae 'αὐτὸ τὸ . . .' and '. . . αὐτὸ καθ' αὐτό',[1] 'the . . . itself' and '. . . alone by itself'.

The roots of the notion of essence are in Anaxagoras, a central thesis of whose system was that there are portions of opposites, such as 'the large' and 'the small', in everything, and that only Mind exists alone by itself and unmixed.[2] To propound a thesis of this sort is to prompt consideration of its denial. If the opposites are always mixed together, what would it be like for them to be unmixed, ἐφ' ἑαυτοῦ, alone and by themselves? To ask this sort of question is to take a long step towards asking the kind of question the *Euthyphro* asks about holiness. There is evidence in Aristophanes, though it is not strong, that the historical Socrates took that step, that he used the formula 'αὐτὸ καθ' αὐτό', and therefore presumably the thought that lay behind it.[3] And Xenophon testifies that he asked the question, 'What is it?':[4]

He himself never wearied of discussing human topics: What is piety? What is impiety? What is the beautiful? What the ugly? What the noble? What the base? What are meant by just and unjust? ... and other like problems, the knowledge of which, as he put it, conferred a patent of nobility on the possessor, whereas those who lacked the knowledge might deservedly be stigmatized as slaves.

It does not follow from this, of course, that the historical Socrates intended the 'What is it?' question to be circumscribed in

[1] These formulae are typical in the middle dialogues, but rare earlier; see, however, αὐτὸ τὸ εἶδος, *Euthyphro*, 6d, 10, and τὸ ὅσιον αὐτὸ αὐτῷ, 5d 2.

[2] Of the large and small, Anaxagoras says: οὐδὲ χωρὶς ἔστιν εἶναι, ἀλλὰ πάντα παντὸς μοῖραν μετέχει. (*DK*, Fr. 6). Mind, on the other hand, is μόνον ἐόντα ἐφ' ἑαυτοῦ. (*DK*, Fr. 12). It is worth noticing, here and elsewhere, the degree to which Anaxagoras anticipated Plato's own philosophical vocabulary. This was not the only way in which he influenced Plato's prose: see J. D. Denniston, *Greek Prose Style*, pp. 3–5.

[3] *Clouds*, 194: αὐτὸς καθ' αὐτὸν ἀστρονομεῖν διδάσκεται. This is evidence that the expression 'αὐτὸ καθ' αὐτό' is Socratic, but not irrefragible evidence. Aristophanes uses the masculine rather than the neuter; he would have found the concept, and a close approximation to the phrase, in Anaxagoras; the Socrates of the *Clouds* is meant to represent 'the wise' generally, and Socrates himself, so to speak, only accidentally; and the joke fits Anaxagoras, who was concerned about astronomy and famous for thinking the Moon was Earth, better than it does Socrates, who at least in later life (the *Clouds* was produced in 423, when Socrates was in his late forties) was not so concerned.

[4] *Memorabilia*, I, i, trans. H. G. Dakyns; cf. I, iv, IV, vi.

precisely the way that the *Euthyphro* suggests. But neither does the denial follow. It is at least possible that the dialogue, in its search for essence, for a definition of holiness as it is in itself, represents the mind of the historical Socrates with some accuracy.

As essences, Forms play a regulative role in dialectic. They rule out of court certain kinds of answer to the 'What is it?' question – namely, all those answers which merely offer a distinguishing mark characterizing things which have the Form, as distinct from a definition of the Form itself. You cannot say what a characteristic is as such by merely offering a mark for distinguishing its instances. *Euthyphro*, 10e–11a, is a palmary example of this. It is perhaps true that the holy is loved by all the gods: but this states only a πάθος of holiness, not its οὐσία. Again, Socrates later infers that if the holy is what is acceptable to the gods, then it is not what is loved by the gods (15b); this inference makes no sense unless the 'is' involved is the 'is' of definition, not of characterization, answering to οὐσία rather than to πάθος. It is of the essence of dialectic to search for essence.

Mr. Richard Robinson maintains that there is a duality in the 'What is it?' question, or, as he calls it, the question, 'What-is-X?':[1]

> On the one hand, it is merely the search for an equivalent of X, for any description convertible therewith. On the other hand, it is the search for something felt to be narrower than this, for one special equivalent of X which is felt to be X in a more intimate way than any others.

The duality which Mr Robinson suggests consists in the fact that though Socrates sometimes expects to be told the nature or essence of X, he is at other times satisfied with a convertible description of X, a distinguishing mark which will set off all and only X from other Xs. This duality is thought to exist because Socrates has not distinguished between essence and identification, or because he confused them.

One argument Mr Robinson offers in support of this will serve as an example:[2]

> Many passages suggest that all he [Socrates] wants is a mark that shall serve as a pattern by which to judge of any given thing whether

[1] *PED*, p. 57.
[2] *PED*, p. 54.

it is X or not. In the *Euthyphro* (6e) he describes his aim in just this way.

But he does not describe his aim in just this way. He describes it rather as that of learning τὴν ἰδέαν τίς ποτέ ἐστιν of holiness, which he expects to use as a standard or παράδειγμα for determining what things are holy and what are not – no mention of 'mark'. An account of that standard, which is holiness itself, must state its οὐσία, its nature and reality. Mr Robinson had earlier described a critical fallacy which he called 'misinterpretation by inference';[1] his assumption that Socrates wishes only a distinguishing mark at *Euthyphro*, 6e, is a species of that genus, with the difference that it is inference based on no implication. The inference is the less satisfactory because Mr Robinson supposes that Socrates, at *Meno*, 74d, is seeking essence on the ground that he is seeking, '. . . the form of X, the one in the many, that single identical something whose presence in all the many Xs is guaranteed precisely by the fact that we call them all Xs'.[2] Leaving aside the last clause – what is present in things is surely not guaranteed by what we call them – this is an admirable statement of Socrates' aim in *Euthyphro*, 6d–e. But it is an unsatisfactory method of interpretation that enables one to infer from one passage that Socrates is not seeking an essence, *though* he is seeking a Form, and from another that Socrates is seeking an essence *because* he is seeking a Form.

Mr Robinson also offers the following as an argument that there is duality in the Socratic question:[3]

> It is suggested by a word he [Socrates] often uses to describe the process of answering a What-is-it question, namely *horizein*. For this term, never losing the feel of its original connection with boundary-stones, suggests laying down a mark to distinguish a field from the next, without in any way describing the soils or the crops in the fields so delimited. And in Plato's dialogues, the translations 'distinguish' or 'mark off' are suitable as often or more often than 'define'.

But the question is as to the particular kind of marking off

---

[1] *PED*, p. 2.

[2] *PED*, p. 55.

[3] *PED*, p. 55. There are three other arguments offered as well; they each seem to involve either what Mr. Robinson has called 'mosaic' interpretation (p. 2), or a species of 'misinterpretation by inference'.

Socrates intended for his question. The answer of the early dialogues is clear: the boundary-stone is essence.

This conclusion is also implied by the fact that Forms are standards, and by the peculiar priority, which Mr Robinson has himself drawn attention to,[1] of the 'What is it?' question to other questions. Just as one cannot know what things are holy without knowing what holiness is, so one must know what holiness is before one can determine what properties are connected with it. One must know the nature of X before one can know that X is Y.[2] Thus, unless one knows what virtue is, one cannot consult with anyone as to how best to acquire it (*Laches*, 190b–c). Unless one knows what justice is, one cannot know whether it is a virtue, or whether it is profitable, or whether it makes its possessors happy (*Republic*, I, 354b–c). Socrates and Protagoras cannot agree on whether virtue is teachable, or whether it is knowledge, because they do not know what virtue is (*Protagoras*, 359e–361d). Because Socrates does not know what virtue is, he cannot say what its properties are (ὁποῖόν τι), or specifically, whether it is taught or acquired by practice or present by nature (*Meno*, 71b), How, indeed, could one determine ποῖόν τί ἐστι without knowing ὅ τι ἔστι?[3]

What does all this imply? It implies that knowledge of οὐσία is prior to knowledge of πάθος, that unless one knows what holiness is in that 'intimate' sense of which Mr Robinson speaks, one cannot know what properties are connected with it. If the early dialogues exhibited the duality Mr Robinson claims for them, they would be sadly incoherent. But, in fact, there is priority, not duality, in their treatment: essence is the lynch-pin of knowledge.

The priority of οὐσία to πάθος is directly implicated with the fact that Forms are standards. The ground of connection of any property of holiness must lie either in the nature of holiness itself or in things which are holy: that holiness is teachable, for example, is either a claim about the Form of holiness or about

---

[1] *PED*, pp. 50–1.

[2] This claim should not be confused with a different one. One can certainly know that there is something in the closet without knowing that it is a horse; but it is not equally clear that one can know that virtue is (say) teachable unless one knows what virtue is. An essence is a nature, not a thing which has a nature.

[3] *Meno*, 86e. For the results of trying, see 100b. Notice that the question ποῖόν τι is *not* contrasted with τί in the *Euthyphro*. See above, p. 69, n. 1.

those things in which the Form is present. In either case, one cannot estimate its truth without knowing what holiness is, since one must know what holiness is before one can determine what things are holy. This explains why the question, 'What is holiness?' cannot be answered with properties or πάθη connected with holiness; that sort of answer would involve a circle. To ask, 'What is holiness?' is to ask, not that holy things be characterized, but that holiness be defined.

2. REAL DEFINITION

The 'What is it?' question, in the dialectic of the early dialogues, has a determinate and technical sense. The answer to it must specify a Form – that is, a universal, standard, and essence. The *Euthyphro* suggests that that specification must state what whole that Form is part of, and what part of the whole it is: to answer the question, 'What is the holy?' is to define holiness by genus and difference.

The kind of definition here in view is, of course, real definition, not nominal definition; it is definition not of words which are true of things, but of the nature of those things of which words are true. Real definition is analysis of essence, rather than stipulation as to how words shall be used or a report as to how they are in fact used. Because it is analysis of essence, real definition is, as stipulation is not, either true or false. For example, it is true that justice is a virtue, and false that it is a quantity, and this remains so if the *is* is construed as a definitional *is* relating species and genus.

One common notion of real definition is that it is merely nominal definition plus an existence claim. Thus, for example, the real definition of triangle would be: 'Triangle means "plain three-angled figure", and there are triangles'. Mill argued this in the last century,[1] and, according to some interpreters, it was also Aristotle's view. Thus Sir Thomas Heath wrote:[2]

> There is nothing in connexion with definitions which Aristotle takes more pains to emphasize than that a definition asserts

[1] J. S. Mill, *System of Logic*, I, viii; see also W. Kneale and M. Kneale, *The Development of Logic*, pp. 373-4.
[2] T. L. Heath, *Euclid's* Elements, vol. i, p. 143; cf. 117-24; see also *History of Greek Mathematics*, vol. i, p. 337.

nothing as to the *existence* or *non-existence* of the thing defined. It is an answer to the question *what* a thing is, and does not say *that* it is. The *existence* of the various things defined has to be proved, except in the case of a few primary things in each science, the existence of which is indemonstrable and must be *assumed* among the first principles of each science; e.g. points and lines in geometry must be *assumed* to exist, but the existence of everything else must be *proved*.

Heath proceeds to connect Aristotle's theory, which is probably more closely related to the mathematics of his time than has generally been recognized, with Euclid's practice in the *Elements*, where construction functions as a proof of existence:[1]

(S)peaking generally, Euclid's definitions, and his use of them, agree with the doctrine of Aristotle that the definitions themselves say nothing as to the existence of the things defined, but that the existence of each of them must be proved or (in the case of the 'principles') *assumed*. In geometry, says Aristotle, the existence of points and lines only must be assumed, the existence of the rest being proved. Accordingly Euclid's first three postulates declare the possibility of constructing straight lines and circles (the only 'lines' except straight lines used in the *Elements*). Other things are defined and afterwards constructed and proved to exist: e.g. in Book I, Def. 20, it is explained what is meant by an equilateral triangle; then (I, 1) it is proposed to construct it, and, when constructed, it is proved to agree with the definition. When a square is defined (I, Def. 22) the question whether such a thing really exists is left open until, in I, 46, it is proved to satisfy the definition. Similarly with the right angle (I, Def. 10, and I, 11) and parallels (I, Def. 23, and I, 27–9). The greatest care is taken to exclude mere presumption and imagination. The transition from the subjective definition of names to the objective definition of things is made, in geometry, by means of *constructions* (the first principles of which are postulated), as in other sciences it is made by means of experience.

This account of definition and existence undoubtedly was known in the Academy, where Aristotle would have learned it. It may have its roots in Plato's method of inquiry by hypothesis, which allowed one to assume the existence of something of a certian nature, and then to support or reject the assumption.[2] Aristotle

---

[1] Heath, *op. cit.*, p. 146.
[2] Cf. *Phaedo*, 100a–e, 101c–d.

was not the first to insist that 'What is meant by a unit and the fact that a unit exists are different things'.[1]

This view of real definition also conforms closely to the account of the relation between existence and analyticity often offered in modern logical theory. Definitions, or more accurately, statements whose truth rests solely on definitions, are analytic, true in virtue of the meaning of their terms, and their denials are self-contradictory. Thus, 'Vixens are female foxes', for example, is true precisely because the expression 'vixen' is synonymous with the expression 'female fox': to verify it, we look not to the world, but to the language in which we talk about the world. But no analytic statement implies, as analytic, an existence claim: to suppose this would be to suppose that existence can be part of the meaning of a predicative expression, and is itself a predicate, whereas in fact it is a quantifier specifying the application of predicates. Thus the meaning of 'vixen' does not and cannot imply that there are vixens: for that piece of information we must look, not to the language in which we talk about the world, but to the world.

The view that real definition is simply nominal definition plus an existence claim has both the weight of centuries of mathematical and philosophical tradition behind it, and the weight of contemporary logical theory. It requires an act of intellectual imagination to see that it is not the view assumed in the *Euthyphro* and other early dialogues.

And assuredly it is not. The dialectical procedure of the *Euthyphro* cannot be represented as an attempt to discover what the word 'holy' means, coupled with a further attempt to find out whether it applies to anything. For, in the first place, the requirements for answering the 'What is it?' question are not those of nominal definition: nominal definitions are definitions of words, not of standards or of essences, and there is no good reason why they should be required always to be *per genus et differentiam*. And, in the second place, existential import is taken for granted, not demonstrated, in the early dialogues: Socrates and Euthyphro assume that there are holy things, and ask only what their nature is; and this assumption of existence is made in every early dialogue in which that 'What is it?' question is initially

[1] *Post. Anal.*, I, 72a, 24.

81

answered by appeal to examples – which is to say in every early dialogue in which it is asked.

This may be summarized in another way. A Form is not a 'hypostatized meaning', for there may be expressions which mean but have no application – 'goat-stag' and 'squared circle', for example. A Form is not a 'possibility', or a Whiteheadean eternal object, since there may be possibilities which nothing satisfies – as witness unicorns. A Form is rather the nature of something which is, and existential import is therefore built into the very notion of it; the question of whether there are Forms which nothing has rests on confusion.[1]

For Socratic dialectic, existence is, so to speak, a given: the aim is to penetrate its nature, and that penetration will be expressed in a definition. If this view were generalized, transferred from questions about ethics and conduct to questions about the world at large, definition would become the foundation of all knowledge of what is.

In the early dialogues, real definition is an account of an object – an object which serves as the goal of inquiry. And in this connection it is perhaps worth observing that if such definition is not definition of a word, neither is it definition of a 'concept'. Euthyphro's conception of holiness, or what the ordinary Athenian ordinarily understood by the word 'holiness', is inadequate to the nature and essence of holiness; this is shown by *elenchus*, dialectical refutation. The relation of our ordinary concepts to Forms is in some sense teleological: the Form of holiness is presumably what Euthyphro would understand by the world 'holiness' if he fully understood the meaning of his words. The *Protagoras* suggests as a possibility that he would then realize that he meant exactly the same thing by the word 'holiness' that he meant by such other words as 'justice', 'courage', 'temperance', 'wisdom', and 'virtue', though inspection of these words in their everyday use would suggest only that this was a paradox. What we ordinarily understand by a word is not necessarily what we ought to understand by it, and the distinction between Forms and our ordinary concepts explains both the need for and the difficulty of real definition. Considerable education and much reflection are required to prevent the incautious

---

[1] Cf. *Post. Anal.*, II, 92b, 3–12, *Meta.*, VII, 1031a, 12 ff.

identification of the nature of things with our notions of the nature of things.

Genus and Difference

Definition, according to textbooks of traditional logic,[1] proceeds by citing a genus common to many species, and a difference which marks off the species under examination from all others. It is so in Aristotle, for example, and Professor Ross has argued that it is also so in the early dialogues:[2]

> It is implied [by such questions as 'What is courage?'] that courage is a complex thing capable of being analysed into elements; for if it were not so, the question ... would be a stupid one, the only true answer being that courage is courage. The answers which from time to time he [Socrates] gives to questions of this form show that in principle he was assuming, as Aristotle proceeded to do explicitly, that definition is analysis *per genus et differentiam*.

The claim that definition is to proceed through genus and difference is confirmed by the *Euthyphro*. Socrates' discussion of the matter falls into two parts. The first suggests that definition must provide a genus: it asks whether the holy is part of the just, and the just not part of the holy, as reverence is a part of fear, while fear is not, as Stasinus is made to claim,[3] a part of reverence. Socrates next proceeds to introduce, without labelling it, the notion of difference; this new stage in the argument is explicitly marked by his call to 'consider the next point' (12d, 5): if the holy is part of the just, the next thing to find out is what part it is, as even number is that part of number with equal rather than unequal sides.

Not all examples of definition in the early dialogues offer genus and difference.[4] In the *Laches* (192b), for example, quickness is defined as 'the power of getting a lot done in a little time', and in the *Meno* (75b) figure is at first defined as 'what always follows colour'. Neither definition satisfies the *Euthyphro*'s requirements. But the *Meno* proceeds to improve the definition of figure by defining it as 'the limit of a solid' (76a), which gives genus and

---

[1] See H. W. B. Joseph, *Introduction to Logic* (2nd ed.), p. 112.
[2] *PTI*, p. 12; see also *PED* (2nd ed.), p. 58.
[3] See above, p. 49, n. 1.
[4] And it may be added that most of Euclid's definitions in the *Elements* do not.

difference; so, perhaps, does the jingling sham definition, offered in the manner of Gorgias, which defines colour as 'an effluence of figure commensurable with sight' (76d).

It remains uncertain whether Socrates' account of definition in the *Euthyphro* is his final account of the matter, or whether his remarks are in part meant dialectically, as a means of bringing Euthyphro along. There is evidence for the latter view. If holiness is a part of justice, as reverence is a part of fear, then, by Euthyphro's account, justice is broader than holiness, as fear is broader then reverence; that is, while holiness implies justice, justice does not imply holiness. This conflicts with the famous Socratic thesis, maintained in the *Protagoras* and implicit in other early dialogues, that virtue is one – one either in the sense that all virtues are the same in definition, or in the sense that they are all mutually implicatory. It may be, therefore, that, at least in the special case of virtue, Socrates' account of definition in the *Euthyphro* is not one which he would have accepted without qualification, and requires emendation: to say that *a* is part of *b* need not always imply that *b* is found in more places than *a*.

This does not alter the fact that the *Euthyphro* envisages definition as *per genus et differentiam*. But the *Euthyphro* does not support Professor Ross's suggestion that the *definiendum* must be 'a complex thing capable of being analysed into elements'. This suggestion is liable to the general objection that it implies that definition must either terminate in a set of items which are simple in the sense that they are indefinable, in which case holiness, for example, is composed of elements, but it is impossible to say what those elements are; or it implies an infinite regress, one which does not terminate, in which case definition is impossible, in that one cannot say what anything is. Nor is there textual support for Professor Ross's interpretation; Socrates' metaphors of spatial overlap in no way suggest the divisibility of species; the inference drawn from the fact that fear is everywhere that reverence is, but reverence is not everywhere that fear is is not that fear is a part of reverence, but that reverence is a part of fear; one does not divide reverence and get fear, but in examining reverence one finds that it implies fear. As with genus, so with difference. The example of difference given is that even number is 'number with equal rather than unequal sides', that is, number which is integrally divisible by two. Since two is itself even, however, this difference expresses a necessary consequence of the existence of even number, not an element in the constitution of even number. The assumption that definition implies that the *definiendum* must be 'a complex thing capable of being analysed into elements' represents a projection of the Aristotelian account of definition on to the text of the *Euthyphro*. That projection is mistaken.

Aristotelian Genera

The ordinary connotations of 'genus' and 'species' are Aristotelian connotations. Aristotle thought, and the deposit of logical tradition derived from him assumes, that genera are poorer in content than species, and that passage upward in the abstractive hierarchy is passage toward emptiness. Each species in the Tree of Porphyry implies its proximate, subaltern, and *summum* genera, since they are involved in its definition.[1] But no genus implies the species which fall under it. Thus, man implies animal, but animal does not imply man; animal, in turn, implies but is not implied by living thing. The genus has fewer *merkmale*, fewer notes, than the species; it is conceptually poorer.

Ascent toward emptiness, descent toward fullness. This account of the relation of species to genera has often been treated as a neutral matter of logic. But it is by no means so neutral a procedure as it has been made to appear: it involves metaphysics.

It is often supposed that Aristotle looked out on his world one day and discovered individuals – the first of a mighty line of philosophers possessed of what has been called 'a robust sense of reality'. Perhaps so. But there is evidence that he rather looked out and discovered natural kinds – discovered the primacy not of Socrates, but of man, not of Dobbin, but of horse – and that it was through this discovery of natural kinds that he was led to sponsor the ontological primacy of such individuals as Socrates and Dobbin, who are *of* those kinds. The road to this discovery passed through a thicket of controversy over definition in the Academy, involving not only Plato, but Speusippus.[2] It issued in the doctrine of the *Categories* that the distinguishing mark of

---

[1] See H. W. B. Joseph, *Introduction to Logic* (2nd ed.), pp. 130-1; see also F. H. Bradley, *Principles of Logic*, vol. i, Oxford, 1883, p. 172.

[2] See *REA*, ch. ii, especially pp. 37-43.

secondary substance – that is, predicates in the category of substance – is that they are predicable in name and definition.[1] This rule, which is meant to enable one to pick out terms which express the nature of basic realities, is tied to ontology:[2]

> Of the secondary substances the species is more a substance than the genus, since it is nearer the primary substance. For if one is to say of the primary substance what it is, it will be more informative and apt to give the species than the genus. For example, it would be more informative to say of the individual man that he is a man than that he is an animal (since the one is more distinctive of the individual man, while the other is more general); and more informative to say of the individual tree that it is a tree than that it is a plant. Further, it is because the primary substances are subject for all other things and all other things are predicable of them or are in them, that they are called substances most of all. But as the primary substances stand to the other things, so the species stands to the genus: the species is a subject for the genus (for genera are predicated of the species, but the species is not predicated reciprocally of the genera). Hence for this reason too the species is more a substance than the genus.

This passage puts forward, for the first time in the history of philosophy, the doctrine of generic emptiness. It also explains its underpinning. Aristotle construes the relation of species to genus as predicative, and predication is asymmetrical: the genus is predicable of its species, but neither species nor difference is predicable of the genus: man is an animal, but animal is neither man nor two-legged. Since genera stand to species as species stand to individuals, and since individuals are more substance than species, species are more substance than genera, even though species and genera are both secondary substances, in contrast to the primary substance of which they are predicable, such as Socrates or Coriscus. Granting all this, the impoverishment of genera follows immediately: genera, which are relatively less substance, can hardly contain species, which are relatively more. Put logically, genera cannot imply species because the differences of species must be extrinsic to their genera, in that they are impredicable of their genera: the genus does not imply its species because it is only one element in the analysis of that

[1] *Categories*, 3a, 7 ff; cf. 2a, 19 ff.
[2] *Categories*, 2b, 7 ff., trans. Ackrill.

86

species. The asymmetry of predication in the relation of genus to species implies asymmetry of implication.

The *Categories* is an early work, and Aristotle's vocabulary changed as his mind grew. The contrast between primary and secondary substance was later abandoned; primary substance dissolved into matter, form, and their compound; secondary substance into substantial form and universal. But the assumption that genera are more empty than species remained. In the *Metaphysics*, by a metaphor, genera become as matter for species, potencies for further determination to which differences stand relatively as form.[1]

This claim, or something like it, has coloured most subsequent thought on universals. It assumes the primacy of individuals as logical subjects, the primacy of things of which things are said and are not themselves said of anything; and it assumes the derivativeness of predicates, things which are said of other things. These are not Platonic assumptions.

Platonic Genera

Aristotle's account of genera does not fit the early dialogues. To begin with, though it keeps to Socrates' vocabulary, it reverses his metaphor. Socrates held that the species is a *part* of the genus, which is a whole – a whole which contains this part plus other parts. But if genera are more impoverished than species, it is the species which is the whole, of which genus and difference are the respective parts.[2] Aristotle was led to sponsor this reversal of metaphor by reflection on problems inherent in theories of definition in the Academy; but is is unlikely that Socrates, who first introduced the metaphor of part and whole, introduced it as reversed.

There is a second difficulty in the way of matching impoverished genera with the early and the middle dialogues. It is that they do not fit the kinds of term Socrates there has primarily in view. The Tree of Porphyry narrows as it rises. This is well enough for the relation of man to animal, or animal to living thing. But it is not well enough for the relation of even number to number, or circle to figure, or justice to virtue. For it is reasonable to suppose that

[1] *Metaphysics*, VIII, 1045a, 20 ff.; cf. 1938a, 19.
[2] Cf. *Metaphysics*, V, 1023b, 23-5.

the existence of number implies the existence of even number; that the existence of figure implies the existence of circular figure; that the existence of virtue implies the existence of justice as a virtue. The doctrine of generic impoverishment, if it suits anything, suits natural kinds, such as horse and dog. That is why Aristotle sponsored it. But it does not suit mathematical terms, or moral terms, and therefore it does not suit the dialectic of the early dialogues.[1] To suppose it paradigmatic for the notion of definition is to ignore the actual structure of concepts; and it is a melancholy testimony to the power of false abstraction over the human mind that such a view of genera should have been so long, and so widely, accepted.

The role of difference in definition will change as genera are regarded alternatively as rich or impoverished. If the latter, difference becomes the final determination of the species: 'The *last* differentia will be the substance of the thing and its definition.'[2] The species will contain as parts its genus and its difference,[3] and it will be definitionally identical with its parts, in the sense that they are in conjunction what it is. But if genera are conceived as wholes which contain their species as parts, difference must play a different role; for, since the whole is itself constituted of its parts, there is no determination which, added to the whole, will constitute a part. Put in another way, difference will be a character by means of which one species may be distinguished from others in the same genus; but it will be a consequence of that

[1] An excellent example of the richness of implication of genera in the later dialogues is found in the *Timaeus*, where the Intelligible Living Creature on which the world is modelled contains all the intelligible living creatures that there are (*Timaeus*, 31a; cf. *PC*, p. 41, n. 1; see also *Sophist*, 253d, and *PTK*, pp. 263–73, especially pp. 268 ff.).

Coupled with the doctrine of generic impoverishment, it may be added, is the doctrine of the exclusivity of species. The species of natural things are exclusive: no goat is a stag. Neither, to carry the story further, is any odd number even. But Plato surely thought that the nature of a holy act as holy might also imply that it is just. The doctrine of the Unity of Virtue implies that one cannot assume in advance, as Aristotle was wont to do throughout the categories, that species exclude each other.

[2] *Metaphysics*, VII, 1038a, 19. The point is that though rationality, say, is not the species man, rationality *as difference of animal* is the species man. Cf. VIII, 1045a, 20 ff.

[3] Though, to be sure, Aristotle conceived those parts, for reasons stemming from the problem of the unity of definition, as parts of different ontological orders, standing to each other as potentiality to actuality, or matter to form.

distinction rather than constitutive of it; it will be a *ratio cogno-scendi*, not a *ratio essendi*. Thus, for example, divisibility by two is an essential difference between odd and even number; it does not, however, *constitute* the distinction between odd and even number, but is rather a necessary *consequence* of that distinction.

Definability and Simplicity

There is no satisfactory definition of a virtue in any early dialogue.[1] From this it has often been inferred, not that the attainment of real definition is difficult, as no doubt it is, but that it is impossible: Forms cannot in principle be defined.

To infer from the fact that satisfactory definitions are not reached to the conclusion that they cannot be reached is a logical solecism; nor can it be explained why, if Plato and Socrates believed that Forms were not definable, they should have sponsored a method of dialectical inquiry which assumed that they are. If Forms cannot be defined, the 'What is it?' question cannot in principle be answered. That is, it is a nonsense question. But why then should it have been asked? Why should Socrates imply at *Euthyphro*, 14c, that it can be answered? And why should he have supposed that until it is answered the answers to many other questions, for example, questions of ποῖόν τι, cannot be known? – that the question 'What is virtue?' is prior to the question 'Can virtue be taught?' Few claims about the early dialogues are so ill grounded as the claim that Forms cannot be defined.

But if Forms are definable, the problem remains of reconciling their definability with their simplicity.

Consider a problem which troubled Aristotle, the problem of the unity of definition.[2] There is a species, S, which is to be defined in terms of a genus, G, and a difference, D. That is, S is G and D, and the *is* is the *is* of definitional identity, since GD is what S is. But this generates a paradox: for there is one thing mentioned in the *definiendum*, and two in the *definiens*. But how can one thing be identical with two things? How can S *be* G and D?

---

[1] It has been suggested that the definition of courage at *Protagoras*, 360d, is meant as final; but see *Protagoras*, 360e–361c.

[2] See *De Interpretatione*, 17a, 13, 20b, 15, *Metaphysics*, 1015b, 16–1017a, 6, 1037b, 8 ff., 1945a, 7 ff. For further discussion, with review of ancient testimony, see *ACPA*, pp. 38 ff.

If the definition in view were merely nominal, this problem would be uninteresting. The *is* would be the *is* of synonymy, and there is no reason why a complex expression should not be synonymous with another expression which is, relatively to it, linguistically more simple. But the definition here in view is not nominal, but real, and the paradox it generates is also real. Aristotle attempted to solve it in the *Metaphysics* by his doctrine that being is ambiguous between potentiality and actuality. Species, genus and difference are all things which are; genus, however, is in itself only a kind of matter or potentiality, to which difference stands relatively as actuality and form.

Whatever the merits of this solution, it is irrelevant to Plato's early dialogues. A Form, which is one thing, cannot be identical with any other Form or set of Forms distinct from it, and definition therefore, cannot express an identity of the sort Aristotle intends. Socrates could not consistently have supposed that asking the 'What is it?' question of a virtue implies that the inner being of that virtue is complex, and contains the genus virtue, and a difference, as constituents in its complexity. Relative to definition, species are simple units, and the problem of the unity of definition, at least as posed by Aristotle, does not arise.

But it may well be asked whether another problem does not take its place. If species are simple units, how can they be defined at all? This difficulty, though it has been widely canvassed, is more apparent than real. Simplicity and complexity are relative terms. Nothing is *just* simple or *just* complex; it is simple or complex in given respects, and may be otherwise in other respects. If virtue is a whole of which holiness is a part, and if holiness stands to no inferior Form as virtue stands to holiness, then virtue is complex and holiness simple in respect to having parts. But if Forms of species are in this respect simple, it hardly follows that they are in every respect simple; the very argument by which their simplicity is established implies that they stand in relations of part and whole, difference, implication, and compatibility with other Forms. They are not windowless monads, and an account can be given of them.[1] They are definable by tracing their relations

---

[1] See *Phaedrus* 270d. It has sometimes been denied, on the strength of later dialogues, that an account can be given of Forms. One text used to support this view is *Parmenides*, 129d–e, which has been taken to imply that Forms cannot combine with

to the broader Forms which contain them. Those broader Forms, which are genera, are complex in respect of having parts; but once again, from the fact that genera are complex in this respect, it does not follow that they are complex in every respect; it may be that genera are simple in respect to their containment by higher genera, as being wholes which are more than the sum of their parts.[1]

The Structure of the Realm of Forms

If the relation of species to genus is founded on the structure of Forms, that structure must be a hierarchy.

This is a widely accepted view;[2] but it has met with opposition. Professor Cherniss, for example, holds that it is false:[3]

> No idea is to any other as a constituent part to a whole or as a genus to its species.... Nor does Plato anywhere make the distinction of genus and species among the ideas; but what Aristotle calls genus, differentia, and species are for him all distinct ideal units, each

[1] Cf. *Theaetetus*, 204a.
[2] See *PTK*, pp. 268–73.
[3] *REA*, p. 54; cf. *ACPA*, n. 128 and pp. 46–8.

---

one another. But, in fact, that text does not imply this, but only that Forms cannot combine with their own opposites.

Another text bearing on the issue is *Theaetetus*, 201, the 'Dream of Socrates'. It has been held that since Forms are simple proper nameables, Plato when he wrote the *Theaetetus* must have come to see that no account of them is possible, and thus when Socrates refutes the view that there may be knowledge of complexes whose constituents are simple and unknowable, he is refuting the Theory of Forms. (See G. Ryle, 'Plato's *Parmenides*', *SPM*, pp. 107–8; see also R. C. Cross, 'Logos and Forms in Plato', *ibid.*, pp. 190 ff.) On the other hand, *Theaetetus* 201 has been held to imply something very different – namely, that since simples can have no account given of them, and Forms are susceptible of account, Forms must have been latently complex all along. (See *PED*, p. 58; Mr Robinson appears to hold a different view in *Philosophical Review*, lix (1950), p. 16.)

Both conclusions share an identical premise: that simplicity in Forms is incompatible with an account being given of them. But Wittgenstein's remark is relevant here: ' "Simple" means: not composite. And here the point is: in what sense "composite"? It makes no sense at all to speak absolutely of the "simple parts of a chair"'. (*Philosophical Investigations*, para. 47). The theory dreamt up by Socrates in the *Theaetetus* is not the theory of Forms, for every dialogue which aims at definition assumes that Forms are intentionally related – assumes, in effect, a communion of kinds (see *ACPA*, n. 128). Such communion does not imply reducibility to simpler constituents.

other than the others, each having aspects which imply the existence of the others or are compatible with them, but each being an independent nature which cannot be exhaustively analysed into the others. Plato could not, then, have intended by the use of diaeresis to produce an ontological hierarchy of the world of ideas. The *Sophist* and *Politicus*, which have come to be considered as handbooks of diaeresis, show that he meant it rather to be a heuristic method, an instrument to facilitate the search for a definite idea, the distinction of that idea from other ideas, and its implications and identification, and that he did not imagine it to be a description of the 'construction' of the idea, its derivation, or its constituent elements.

Professor Cherniss supposes not only that some Forms are simple as having no parts, but that all Forms are in this way simple, and that the realm of Forms is flat. His remarks are aimed at the later dialogues, and specifically at the doctrine of the communion of kinds in the *Sophist*; but they are meant as an interpretation of the early dialogues as well.[1]

The texts against this view are all those texts which state or imply that the answer to the 'What is it?' question will specify a genus or whole of which the Form under examination is a part, or that that Form is a whole which contains parts. Those texts are: *Euthyphro*, 11e–12a, *Protagoras*, 329c ff., *Meno*, 74–6, *Laches*, 190c–d, 199e. All of these passages imply the possibility of subsuming species under genera, and thus a hierarchical arrangement of Forms. They imply that the realm of Forms is not flat, but tiered.

Professor Cherniss proposes that these texts, and others in later dialogues, be set aside on the ground that their purpose is heuristic: they reflect an assumption in method rather than metaphysics. But a method of inquiry is, or should be, fitted to the nature of its subject-matter, and if it is useful for purposes of discovery to suppose that Forms stand to each other as species and genus, it ought to be possible to explain why this is so. The obvious answer is that the assumption answers to the real structure of Forms. Professor Cherniss, rejecting this answer, offers nothing to put in its place. Yet that rejection implies an incommensurability between method and object which needs explanation: How is it possible for the assumption that Forms are subsumable under genera and hierarchically arranged to serve a

[1] See *REA*, pp. 4–6.

heuristic function, when there are in fact no genera and no hierarchy?

There is a further difficulty. In the early dialogues, Plato insists either on the priority of questions of τί to questions of ποῖόν τι or on the distinction between οὐσία and πάθος. But if the only relations among Forms are those of difference, implication, and compatibility, as Professor Cherniss suggests, this distinction cannot be drawn. For then, if the Form F is *not* identified with its implications and compatibilities, the question 'What is F?' cannot be answered: F can be characterized only by its relations, and there is no ground for supposing that certain of those relations are more of its essence than others. There is no ground, therefore, for distinguishing οὐσία from πάθος. On the other hand, if F *is* identified with its implications and compatibilities, the latter became what it is to be F; and if any of them were lacking or other than they are, F would not be what it is, but other than what it is. That is, identification leads to 'internal relations'. And since compatibility and implication relate every Form to every other Form, F will be *essentially* related to every other Form: the Truth will be the Whole. Speusippus appears later to have come very close to taking this step;[1] but Plato, at least in the early dialogues, did not, for it denies that there is a distinction between πάθος and οὐσία.

If the 'What is it?' question is to be asked and answered as Socrates asked and attempted to see it answered, and if it is to be kept distinct from questions of ποῖόν τι, some further connection is needed among Forms than the relations of implication and compatibility and their denials. The nature of that connection is indicated in the *Meno* by the claim that justice is not virtue but *a* virtue, in the *Laches* by the claim that courage is a part of virtue, which is a whole, in the *Euthyphro* by the claim that holiness is a part of justice. The connection is the connection between species and genus: to understand the nature of a part, we must locate its position in the whole of which it is a part.

The Unity of Virtue

The view that the virtues are definable by locating them within a genus seems to run afoul of another early dialogue, the *Protagoras*,

[1] See Aristotle, *Posterior Analytics*, II, 97a, 6–22; see also *REA*, p. 37, and *ACPA*, pp. 59–62 and n. 49.

where Socrates maintains that virtue is one. This thesis was to occupy Plato's thought to the end of his life,[1] and it has often been taken to mean that the virtues are identical. Specifically, the message of the *Protagoras* has been thought to be that all virtues are the same in that they are all reducible to knowledge or wisdom, and the claim that Virtue is Knowledge has been held to be the Socratic definition of virtue. Plainly, it is not definition *per genus et differentiam*, which implies the non-identity of species and genus.

The priority of knowledge, in the *Protagoras*, is forcefully put (352b–c):

> Most people think that knowledge has neither strength nor authority nor power of command; that though a man may have it, it can be overpowered – by anger, by pleasure and pain, sometimes by love, often by fear – as though it were some poor slave, to be dragged about at will by the passions. Is that your view, Protagoras? Or would you not rather agree that knowledge is a thing of beauty and power, invincible; that once a man knows good from evil, nothing on earth can compel him to act against that knowledge – wisdom being sufficient to his aid?

This passage undoubtedly represents Socrates' own belief: virtue is knowledge, in the sense that no one willingly or wittingly does evil.[2]

If knowledge implies virtue, and virtue knowledge, it does not thereby follow that virtue and knowledge are one and the same. An equivalence is not an identity. But this equivalence occurs as part of a broader argument, in which Socrates attempts to lead Protagoras to admit that the virtues are all names for the same thing, that 'courage', 'justice', 'temperance', 'holiness', 'wisdom' and 'virtue' are synonyms (349b–c). In view of this, it is not surprising that the *Protagoras* should have been interpreted to mean that the virtues are identical, and definable as knowledge.

Yet there are difficulties in the way of this. To begin with, though the account identifies virtue and knowledge, it robs that identification of force. It is arbitrary, if the names of the virtues are synonyms, whether the virtues are said to be reducible to wisdom, or whether the virtues, including wisdom, are said to be reducible to holiness or justice or something else. Virtue is

---

[1] See *Laws*, XII, 963a ff.
[2] See also *Meno*, 87c–89a, *Euthydemus*, 278e–282a.

knowledge or wisdom,[1] beyond doubt; but then, virtue is courage or holiness, or what you will, for synonymy is a symmetrical relation.

There is a second difficulty in the way of identification. Socrates in the *Protagoras* offers four arguments against Protagoras' claim that the virtues are distinct. The first (330b–331b) maintains the unity of justice and holiness; the second (332a–333b), the unity of temperance and wisdom; the third (333d–334a), which is interrupted without reaching its conclusion, would have maintained the unity of justice and temperance. There follows a lengthy interlude, after which the question is restated (439b–d), and pursued without interruption through the rest of the dialogue; in his final argument, Socrates undertakes to prove the unity of courage and wisdom (349d–360e). If the unity of the virtues is taken to mean the identity of the virtues, each of these arguments is fallacious, and some of them are blatantly and scandalously fallacious. This breaks the back of the dialogue. Protagoras is portrayed throughout as an intelligent man, wise in the ways of words, but unable to deal with Socrates' arguments. His failure is surely not due to lack of skill in verbal gymnastics; one can hardly expect that in a Sophist. It is due to the fact that, although he claims to teach virtue, he does not know what virtue is. Socrates' arguments, if they were mere blank fallacies, would hardly contribute, as they are meant to do, toward indicating this conclusion.

As in other early dialogues, the *Protagoras* ends in failure, and for a familiar reason: Socrates and Protagoras disagree over whether virtue can be taught, without first determining what virtue is. This point is not left to inference: it represents Socrates' explicit summing up of the dialectic of the dialogue (360e–361c):

> I ask these things, I said, for no other reason than a desire to find out how it is with things relating to virtue, and what virtue in itself is. For I know that if that were once shown, the question which you and I have debated, whether virtue can be taught, would be cleared up. As it is, the outcome of the argument might well seem to mock and upbraid us as though it were human; if it had a tongue, it might say, 'What fools you both are, Socrates and Protagoras. You, Socrates, having previously said that virtue

[1] For the equivalence between wisdom and knowledge, compare 330a, 1, and 330b, 4; it is important, when discussing the claim that virtue is knowledge in the *Protagoras*, to bear in mind that knowledge is wisdom, and itself a virtue.

cannot be taught, are now urging just the opposite, trying to show that everything is knowledge – both justice and temperance, and courage – from which it should surely follow that virtue *can* be taught. If it were other than knowledge, as Protagoras tried to claim, then clearly it could not be taught; but now, if it were to prove to be wholly knowledge, as you urge, Socrates, it would be strange indeed if it could not be taught. On the other hand, Protagoras here assumed a while ago that virtue could be taught and seems now to urge the opposite, making it out to be anything but knowledge, so that it would be teachable least of all.' Now, Protagoras, when I see all this agitated back and forth, my desire is to get it cleared up: I should like to sally forth and attack the question, 'What is virtue?' and *then* come back again to ask if it can be taught.

At the conclusion of the *Protagoras*, both Socrates and Protagoras have reversed their positions on the question of whether virtue can be taught. This tangle is a piece of dialectical irony, its purpose not to plead the necessity of finding out what virtue is, but to exhibit it.

The *Protagoras* has a companion piece in the *Meno*. When Socrates is asked by Meno whether virtue can be taught, he undertakes finally to settle the matter by a hypothesis. He assumes that if virtue is knowledge it can be taught (87a–c); argues that it is knowledge (87c–89a); argues that it cannot be taught, since there are no teachers of it (89c–96c); and concludes that it is present in men, 'by divine apportionment, without intelligence' (100a). That is, Socrates assumes an implication, affirms its antecedent, denies its consequent, and ends in scepticism. This structure would be pointless if Plato meant his readers to choose among his premises: the nub of the matter lies elsewhere. Socrates and Meno have tried to settle the question of whether virtue can be taught without first finding out what virtue is. They end in bewilderment, and even the new method of hypothesis (86e–87a), borrowed from the geometers, cannot save them. But then, the geometers can define their terms; Socrates and Meno cannot. This, then, is the lesson of their failure, the familiar Socratic lesson that definition is necessary, that in order to talk it is good to know what one is talking about.[1] The *Meno*, then, is also a piece of dialectical irony: its dramatic structure is meant, not to proclaim, but to exhibit

---

[1] The texts which support this are: 71a–b, 86d–e in conjunction with 99e.

the necessity of definition. It is not concerned to recommend moral conclusions, such as that virtue is knowledge, but to indicate the condition under which such conclusions can alone be reached.

If this is a true account of the *Protagoras* and *Meno*, it militates strongly against the view that the message of the *Protagoras* is the identification of virtue and knowledge. Neither dialogue commits itself to this proposition, and both dialogues emphasize, as the central point of their dialectic, the necessity of answering the question 'What is virtue?' – that is, the necessity of defining it – and suppose at their conclusion that that question has been left unanswered.

It remains to show that Plato's exposition of the problem of the unity of virtue in the *Protagoras* envisages alternate ways in which virtue may be one. Protagoras is led to agree to the following propositions (329c–330b): that virtue is one whole with many parts, which are justice, temperance, holiness, wisdom, and courage; that these parts are distinct, not names for the same thing; that these parts are not parts like the parts of gold, which differ only in size, but parts like the parts of the face, such as eyes and ears, which are of such sort as (οἷον) each other neither in themselves nor in their power or function (οὔτε αὐτὸ οὔτε ἡ δύναμις αὐτοῦ, 330b); and that the parts of virtue are not only distinct, but detachable, in that it is possible for a man to be courageous but unjust or just but unwise, so that he may have some of the virtues without having all.

Protagoras, then, in affirming that virtue is one whole with many parts, is issuing a compound denial: he is denying that the different parts of virtue are the same in themselves; he is also denying that they are the same in power or function. There are two ways, then, in which the virtues may be one.

To say that the virtues differ in themselves is presumably to say that they have different definitions. It is unclear, however, what it means to say that the virtues differ, or are the same, in function. What is the function of a virtue?

That question is nowhere directly answered in the *Protagoras*. The function of a virtue is not the virtue itself, since that makes the example of the face irrelevant: eyes and ears differ from seeing and hearing, which are their functions. Again, one can affirm that two virtues are of such sort as (οἷον) each other without affirming

97

that they are the same (ταὐτόν) or even very similar (ὁμοιότατον).[1] Thus, though the 'function' of a word may be its meaning, or force,[2] and justice is the meaning of 'justice',[3] the function of justice, as distinct from the function of 'justice', is not justice.

If the notion of the function of a virtue is to be understood, we must look to the argument in which the expression is used. The ground on which Protagoras denies that the virtues are the same either in themselves or in their function (330b), and later that they are of such sort as each other (330e–331c), is that they are detachable (329e; cf. 349d). This, then, is to deny that the virtues introduce each other, that the presence of holiness implies the presence of justice, or the presence of courage the presence of wisdom. The inference seems clear: the function of a virtue lies in what it introduces; if the virtues differ in function, they are detachable; if they are detachable, they differ in function.

This fits the pattern of the argument. Protagoras has maintained that the virtues differ *both* in themselves *and* in their function; this proposition will be proved false if it can be shown that the virtues are identical *either* in themselves *or* in their function. If the virtues are one in definition, they are one in function. But it by no means follows that if they are one in function, they are one in definition. It is a different thing to say that a man cannot be holy without being just or just without being holy, or that holiness and justice introduce each other, and to say that the definitions of justice and holiness are the same. The virtues, if detachable, are distinguishable; it does not follow that if they are distinguishable, they are detachable. If the parts of virtue are not parts like the parts of gold, it does not follow that they are parts like the parts of the face, which differ both in themselves *and* in their function. It may be that, in the special case of virtue, the examples both of gold and of the face are inadequate, that there may be difference in definition and sameness in function which neither gold nor the face evince.

So much for the argument. But the dialectical situation is still more complex. If Socrates can show that Protagoras is wrong in

---

[1] 'Very *probably* justice is either the same as holiness or most like it, but it is *beyond question* that justice is of such sort as holiness, and holiness of such sort as justice' (331b, 4–5). For construction, see J. D. Denniston, *The Greek Particles* (2nd ed.), pp. 553–4, and H. W. Smyth, *Greek Grammar*, para. 2858.

[2] See *Cratylus*, 394b.

[3] See *Protagoras*, 329c–d, 349b–c.

supposing that the virtues are detachable, that men can be just without wisdom or courageous without justice, he will have refuted the claim that the virtues differ in themselves and in their function, and shown that the virtues are in *some* sense one. But this is not to show in *what* sense they are one: whether they are one in definition, or one only in that they introduce each other and cannot be detached.

The *Protagoras* maintains a studied ambiguity on this question. It does not choose between the alternatives, and Protagoras himself is unaware of their relevance to the argument. This is not surprising. To ask whether the virtues are one in definition or in function or in both is to ask by implication what virtue is. That question becomes explicit only at the end of the dialogue (361b–c), where Socrates implies that he had it in view all along. But Protagoras, who claimed confidently to be able to teach virtue (318a–319a), and does not know what it is, could not with profit have embarked on an inquiry into its nature until he had gained that conviction of his own ignorance which Socratic *elenchus* was designed to teach.

To sum up: the *Protagoras* envisages two ways in which the virtues may be one – namely, identity or sameness in definition, and mutual implication or sameness in function.[1] This squares with the pattern of argument of other dialogues on the subject, of which the *Meno* gives an excellent specimen:[2]

> We may assert this generally: for man, all other things depend upon the soul, but the things of the soul depend for their goodness on wisdom; by this account, the beneficial is wisdom, and we have said that virtue is beneficial. . . . So we are saying that virtue is wisdom, either wholly or in part.

This argument does not show that wisdom and virtue are identical; it assumes, in fact, that they are distinct. It rather shows that wisdom is a necessary, and also a sufficient, condition for virtue, implies, and is also implied by, the other virtues.

---

[1] See Aristotle, *EN*, V, 1,130a, 9–13, VI, 1,144b, 17–21, VII, 1,145b, 23–35, 1,116b, 4–8. The coimplication of the virtues was maintained by the early Stoa: see H. von Arnim, *Stoicorum Veterum Fragmenta*, vol. iii, pp. 72–4. My thanks are due to Professor C. O. Brink for this reference. See also Diogenes Laertius, VII, 125, and E. R. Dodds, *Gorgias*, p. 335.

[2] *Meno*, 88e–89a; cf. *Protagoras*, 358c–d, *Laches*, 199c–d, *Euthydemus*, 281d–e.

Later, in the *Republic*, Plato offered an account of the virtues founded on an analysis of the soul. That account confirms their unity through mutual implication. The soul will be just when each of its parts performs its proper function; temperate, when each part agrees on which should rule and which obey; wise, when the rational part performs its proper function and rules; courageous, when the spirited part is exercised at its ruler's command (*Republic*, IV, 442b–d). The virtues here clearly differ in definition; equally clearly, they are one in function – they introduce each other, and cannot exist apart from each other. Courage implies wisdom and is implied by it; wisdom implies justice and is implied by it; justice implies temperance and is implied by it. It is not surprising that Socrates should remark in conclusion that, 'Since we have now risen to this height of argument, I seem to see, as from a mountain-top, that there is a single form of virtue.'[1]

The Socratic doctrine of the unity of virtue, then, is not incompatible with the claim that virtue is one whole with many parts, and that the virtues can be defined *per genus et differentiam*. It suggests, however, that the relation between parts and parts, and parts and whole, is coimplicatory.

Logos and Ousia

If the foregoing account is sound, the sort of definition in view in the early dialogues is real and not nominal: it is an account of an object, not an account of a word.[2]

Because that object, at least when it is a species standing in relation to a genus, is simple, the connection which Aristotle held to obtain

---

[1] *Republic*, IV, 445c, trans. F. M. Cornford. It is to be remembered, however, that this account of virtue, and also presumably the tripartite account of the soul with which it is connected, is provisional (see IV, 435d, VI, 504b–505a).

[2] One may imagine an argument to show that there is no difference between real and nominal definition after all. If the meaning of the word 'courage' is courage, and if courage is (say) knowledge of when and when not to be afraid, then it would seem to follow that 'courage' is synonymous with the expression 'knowledge of when and when not to be afraid'. More generally, if S is defined as GD, then 'S' would seem to be synonymous with 'GD'.

The inference is mistaken. It would hold in a language in which the rules of use of concepts conformed to the nature of things: real definition and nominal definition would then coincide. But it does not hold in ordinary Greek or in ordinary English, for in both languages one may meaningfully call a man courageous without attributing wisdom or knowledge to him.

between *definiendum* and *definiens* does not obtain: the species is not a whole identical with its genus and difference as combined parts. But to say that this sort of sameness does not obtain is not to deny that any sort of sameness obtains: at *Euthyphro*, 10d, 13, being loved by the gods is rejected as a definition of holiness because the two are different (ἕτερον; compare the contrary to fact ταὐτόν at 10e, 9), and this rejection is repeated at 15c, 2 (οὐ ταὐτόν . . . ἀλλ' ἕτερα ἀλλήλων).

What sort of sameness is here involved? It is not extensional identity, or substitutibility *salve veritate*, for though all those and only those things loved by the gods are or may be holy, this merely states πάθος, not οὐσία. Nor is it a conceptual identity: Euthyphro, in conceiving of holiness, did not thereby conceive its definition. Nor is it the sameness of synonymy.

Definition is an account of an object. Perhaps, then, the sameness involved in it should be likened to a descriptive identity, the identity of the morning star and the evening star, say, or – to avoid the empirical contingency involved in that example – the identity of the seventh integer with the fourth prime. But this sort of identity implies that two definite descriptions are satisfied by the same object, whereas the *definiendum* of a real definition is not the description of an object, but the object itself. The analogy is closer if a descriptive phrase is replaced by a name: 'Venus is the evening star' or 'Seven is the fourth prime'; it is, after all, plausible to think of definition as a unique description. But this too is misleading. Wisdom, no doubt, is a virtue; but it is mistaken to suppose that '. . . is a virtue' describes wisdom in the same sense that '. . . is virtuous' describes Socrates, for the relation in the first is that of species to genus, and in the second that of an instance of a property to a property. It is the latter relation which is involved in definite description.

It is simplest, perhaps, to say that the sort of identity involved in definition is *sui generis*: it is that identity which obtains when one says *what* a species is, by stating the genus which contains it and a difference which marks it off from other species in the genus. Because species are simple, difference is not constitutive of the distinction of species, but a consequence of that distinction; difference in a definition is a *ratio cognoscendi*, not a *ratio essendi*, and therefore, the identity involved in definition is not an identity of objects. The problem of the unity of definition does not arise.

Perhaps the best analogy for this view of definition – and one which fits many of the connotations of ὁρίζειν and ὅρος – is that of mapping: to define is to locate the position of a species in the genus which contains it. If the species were a farm, the aim of providing a genus would be to indicate the county in which the farm is located; the aim of providing a difference would be, not to survey the boundaries of the farm, but to locate the existence of boundary lines long since surveyed. The sameness involved in definition is, so to speak, the sameness of unique location: the *definiendum* occupies exactly that position mapped in the *definiens*.

Definition *per genus et differentiam*, conceived in this way, involves an assumption in metaphysics. It is that Forms are ranked in a hierarchy, standing to each other as included to what includes, as contained to container. This relation appears to be internal, or mutually constitutive: species depend for their character on their genera, in that they would not be what they are if they were not contained by what contains them; justice, if it were not a virtue, would not be justice. Conversely, virtue, if justice were not a species of it, would not be virtue: the genus depends for its existence and character on its species, the whole on its parts to be the whole it is. Plato is something less than explicit on the point, but presumably definition of genera, unlike definition of species, will involve analysis into constituent parts.

This explains the richness of implication of Platonic genera. For Aristotelian logic, genera are abstractions from species: Socrates and Plato have the common characteristic of being men, and man and horse have the common characteristic of being animals. The genus here is merely an element common to a diversity, more 'abstract' than its species. But if definition is akin to mapping, if genera are wholes containing parts, the genus is not a common characteristic, but, as it were, a system whose existence both presupposes and is presupposed by the existence of its elements or parts. It is because this is so that the genus may be conceived as rich rather than impoverished, as laden with implication rather than comparatively devoid of it.[1]

---

[1] This account should not be confused with Idealist accounts of the 'concrete universal'. Idealism treats the 'concrete' universal as a system of its instances, and condemns genera as merely 'abstract' universals; but since Forms of species are not systems of their instances, while genera are systems (not of instances but of) species, this contrast of concrete and abstract has no application to Plato's views. Again,

As a system, the genus must be possessed of a kind of closure, of a unity which sets it apart from other systems, or other kinds of qualifications. The distinction between οὐσία and πάθος implies a distinction between what is essential to a thing and the characteristics it only *happens* to have. There is a difference between the relation of holiness to justice or virtue, and its relation to being loved by all the gods. If the 'What is it?' question implies internality in essential definition, it also implies that not all accounts of Forms state essence. It implies, that is, externality of relation as well as internality.

Because genera are systems, and species their elements, the definitions of species are maps rather than ordinary statements of identity.[1] To construct such a map, or use it, one can appeal neither to ordinary language nor to individual things and actions: knowledge of Forms will require intellectual intuition, direct

---

[1] Neglect of this point leads to paradox. Thus Professor R. C. Cross, as part of a valuable analysis, writes: 'The move in giving the εἶδος of figure, in answering the question "What is figure?", is to make a statement – "figure is the limit of a solid", and this is regarded as a satisfactory answer. The εἶδος of figure has been displayed in the logos, and displayed in the predicate of the logos. . . . Thus we might say that a form, so far from being "a substantial entity", is more like "a formula". It is the logical predicate in a logos, not the logical subject. It is what is said of something, not something about which something else is said' ('Logos and Forms in Plato', *SPM*, pp. 27–8). But the claim that Forms are 'logical predicates revealed in logoi' assumes that the *definiens* and *definiendum* are identical, rather, than that the *definiens* is a map. Professor Cross's argument is also open to criticism on the basis of the following dilemma: if *definiens* is identical with *definiendum*, as he assumes, then there is not, as he also assumes, a subject-predicate relation between them: the *definiens* is not being said *of* something. On the other hand, if the *definiens* is said of something, and the relation between *definiendum* and *definiens* is that of subject to predicate, the *definiens* is not identical with the *definiendum*. There is, in short, a distinction between predication and identity which the argument seems to neglect. It is also to be observed that there is a distinction between the essence, X-ness, and the essence *of* X-ness; for the question, 'What is the essence of X-ness?' must be answered by a defining formula of the essence, X-ness. Put otherwise, there is a distinction between essence and statement of essence.

Idealism supposes that not merely some but all relations are internal; there is thus only one (ultimate) concrete universal, and it is identical to the one (ultimate) individual, which is Reality. The doctrine of the concrete universal, in short, is nominalism sans plurality, and this also (need one argue?) is without application to Plato's views.

insight into the nature of things which are.[1] The truth of a real definition can be apprehended only by apprehending that of which the definition is an account.[2]

If this is so, then definition and intuition will be mutually supplementary. Intellectual intuition is not to be construed as a specimen, however recondite, of 'knowledge by acquaintance'; one may be acquainted, say, with a patch of blue sky without offering any sort of account of it, for sensation is intellectually effortless. But the intuition of Forms, on the contrary, requires an account; dialectic involves, not merely seeing, but *working* to see, and working to see clearly in a satisfactory account what previously had been seen dimly in an unsatisfactory account. Vision is accomplished by the examination of statements. The comparison of intellectual intuition to knowledge by acquaintance neglects the fact that the object of intellectual intuition is not a given, but a goal.

Some philosophers have claimed to find at this point a strain in Socratic dialectic, a tension between intuition and logic. R. G. Collingwood wrote:[3]

> However highly Plato's philosophical accomplishments are rated, and to rate them at any value short of the highest would be to confess oneself no philosopher, his theory of method must be admitted defective through failure to drive deep enough the distinction established by himself between philosophy and mathematics. The result is that his methodology splits philosophy into

[1] See *Euthyphro*, 6e, *Gorgias*, 503e, *Cratylus*, 389a–c, *Meno*, 72c, *Republic*, X, 596b, *Symposium*, 210–212a. The *Symposium* (212a) combines the metaphor of seeing the Form of beauty with that of touching it; the imagery anticipates that of marriage used at *Republic*, VI, 490a–b.

[2] Notice the effect of this on the notion of analyticity. A proposition is 'analytic' when it is true in virtue of the meaning of its terms, or true by definition. But the notions of meaning and definition are infected by an ambiguity: is the definition in question real or nominal? Suppose that analytic propositions are true by virtue of nominal definition. Then, since what we ordinarily mean by our words may on occasion fail to conform to the nature of things, such propositions may be analytic and false. Thus, for example, it is presumably analytic in Greek that a man may be courageous but not wise, or, to take another example, that no number may be irrational. Suppose then that the definition in question must be real. But real definition is about the world, and about real objects; it is achieved by mapping within genera; it requires the use of intellectual intuition. By all of these criteria, *this* kind of analyticity is 'synthetic'.

[3] *Philosophical Method*, p. 16.

two parts: one an arid waste of ingenious logic-chopping, the other an intuitive vision of ultimate reality. That this first is a pathway to the second may be vouched for by the experience of many generations that have taken Plato for their guide; but even if it is, we are engaged in a philosophical quest, in search not of facts to be accepted on authority, but of conceptions in whose light the facts may be understood; and these Plato has not given us.

This criticism results from forcing intellectual intuition into the mould of sense perception, from failure to realize that, as intellectual, it proceeds through judgement. An act of intellectual insight is not a statement, but it involves a content which is expressible in a statement, and is thereby apt for criticism. A statement is not an act of intellectual insight, but it is that through which insight is expressed – even to oneself.[1] To know is to be able to render an account; to be able to render an account is to know.

But to have reached this point is to have passed beyond the early dialogues.

3. THE EXISTENCE OF FORMS

Socrates in the *Euthyphro* treats the Form of holiness as an existing thing, whose nature he and Euthyphro have set out to discover.[2] This assumption of existence is found in other dialogues as well. In the *Protagoras*, for example, Socrates asks whether justice is or is not a thing (πρᾶγμά τι ἢ οὐδὲν πρᾶγμα),[3] and when Protagoras agrees with him that it is indeed a thing, Socrates goes on to inquire what sort of thing it is. It is further agreed that holiness is a thing, though there is difference of opinion over whether or not it is the same thing as justice. Protagoras had earlier been led by Socrates to say that virtue is a single thing;[4] he will say later that each virtue has its own peculiar nature and reality.[5] In fact, the dialectic of the *Protagoras* turns precisely on an issue of existence (349b–c):

[1] See R. S. Bluck, 'Logos and Forms in Plato', *SPM*, p. 41; see also *PED*, p. 109.

[2] See 5c–d, 6d–e, 11a, 15c–d. See also *Meno*, 71a–b, 86c–d, and *ACPA*, p. 214, n. 128.

[3] 330c; cf. 352d, and καὶ τοῦτο (sc. ὁσιότης) πρᾶγμά τι εἶναι, 330d. See also *Laches*, 192c.

[4] ἕν τι, 329c; cf. *Hippias Minor*, 375d.

[5] τις ἴδιος οὐσία, 349b; cf. *Euthyphro*, 11a, *Hippias Major*, 301b, c, e, 302c.

The question was this: whether 'wisdom', 'temperance', 'courage', 'justice' and 'holiness' are five different names for the same thing, or whether to each of those names there answers a certain nature and reality (οὐσία) peculiar to it, a thing having in each case its own function, none being of such sort as any other. Now, Protagoras, you said that each of those names answers to something peculiar to it, though all are parts of virtue.

The question here is not, Are there any virtues? It is whether there are many virtues or only one. Similarly in the *Euthydemus*, in a passage important for Plato's philosophy of mathematics, geometers, astronomers, and calculators are said to be hunters, since they not only make diagrams, but discover τὰ ὄντα, realities. As hunters, they do not use what they catch, but must turn their prey over to the dialecticians to use properly (290b–c). Again, many of Socrates' analogies would be pointless without an existential assumption – for example, the analogy between virtue and sight drawn in the *Laches*:[1]

> If we know of anything whatever that its addition makes that to which it is added better, and further, if we are able to add it, clearly we must know the thing itself about which we are to become consultants on how one may best and most easily acquire it. Perhaps you don't understand? Look at it this way. If we know that sight added to the eyes makes that to which it is added better, and further, if we are able to add it to the eyes, then clearly we must know the essential nature of sight, about which we are to become advisers on how it may best and most easily be obtained; if one did not know the thing itself, the essential nature of sight or hearing, one could hardly qualify as a consultant or physician in the matter of eyes and ears. . . . But as it is, Laches, our two friends here invite us now to consult about how virtue may be added to the souls of their sons in order to make them better. So the first requirement is to know the essential nature of virtue. For surely, if we do not know what virtue is, we can hardly become consultants as to how best to acquire it.

As sight is to the eyes, and hearing to the ears, so virtue is to the soul. As sight and hearing are things which are, so is virtue a thing which is.

This assumption of existence plays a role in dialectic; more precisely, it explains its point. The aim of dialectic is real definition;

[1] 189e–190b; cf. 191e, 192a–b.

the existential assumption is precisely the assumption that real definitions may be found. A true account of holiness is not arbitrary or subjective, and does not rest on such content as Euthyphro, or anyone else, happens to hold in the forefront of his mind, or on the way he uses words: the true account is an account of the nature of things.

Language and Existence

This interpretation conflicts with the commonly held view that there is no metaphysical commitment to the existence of Forms in the early dialogues, and that talk of Forms there is 'merely a matter of language'. That view seems to confuse language with what language is used to affirm. The Muses may inspire a poet, made drunk by their presence, to compare the redness of a rare sunset to the redness of a rare beefsteak; they do not, or do not thereby, inspire him with the belief that he has added redness along with sunsets and beefsteaks to his ontology. But if that same poet, in more sober mood, were to ask what redness is, explaining that he wished to be told the nature of a characteristic common not only to sunsets and beefsteaks, but to barns, fire-engines, Russians, and all such similar things; if he went on to add that when he learned what it is he expected to use it as a standard for distinguishing what is really red from what is not, and that he expected a proper account of it to state its οὐσία, its nature and reality, and be formulated *per genus et differentian* – if, in short, he laid down rules for real definition and followed them in his inquiry, we should begin to suspect that the inspiration the Muses had visited upon him was metaphysical, rather than poetical, and that he now come equipped with a view of the way the world is and what it contains which goes considerably beyond anything which ordinary language or common sense can show.

The stock objection to this is that, if Socrates' questions had in fact involved a metaphysical assumption about Forms, his respondents would have been unable to answer them.[1] Surely it is significant, it may be argued, that a man like Euthyphro, who, whatever else he is, is no dialectician, should accept without demur the suggestion that there is an ἰδέα of holiness. Surely it is

---

[1] See G. M. A. Grube, *Plato's Thought*, p. 9; for criticism of Grube, see E. A. Havelock, *Preface to Plato*, p. 255.

significant that Protagoras, whom Plato himself portrayed as a conventionalist in morals, is made to agree without hesitation that justice 'is something'. Protagoras can hardly have meant thereby to embrace an ontology of abstract entities; his agreement is more likely to have been prompted by the ordinary uses of language. All of us who are not cynics or otherwise disreputable believe, after all, that there is such a thing as justice.

This objection may be reinforced by pointing to the tendency of ancient Greek to personify abstractions:[1]

> In most Greek prose-writers abstract substantives are seldom made the subject of verbs; the normal agents are human beings. Nevertheless, there are numerous exceptions. . . . It is sometimes difficult to say how far the use of an abstract subject carried with it the idea of personification – in different cases. Perhaps an ancient Greek would have been at a loss for an answer. Nor is it easy to determine how much personification, where it is undoubtedly present, originates in religious or dramatic associations. The abstract subject always, or nearly always, carries with it in Greek some tinge, at least, of personification. We have only to compare Xenophon's phrase (*Mem.*, IV, ii, 39), ἀναγκάζει με καὶ ταῦτα ὁμολογεῖν ἡ ἐμὴ φαυλότης, with the English 'candour compels me to admit', to see how completely in our own language the abstract subject has lost its personifying force. Hence arises a serious difficulty in translating such passages into English, which might partially be met by reviving the eighteenth-century use of initial capitals.

But personification hardly implies metaphysics – even if candour is Candour.

The abstractions Denniston here has in view are nouns such as Sleep, Night, and Digression. It is less easy to see that personification is involved in adjectival abstracts with article or suffix such as 'the holy' or 'holiness', though it may be so.[2] But even if it is not so, it may still be argued that such hypostatization of universals as occurs in the early dialogues involves no genuine ontological commitment. As we may ask what sort of thing a unicorn is without supposing that unicorns exist, so, it may be claimed, we may ask what sort of thing holiness is without supposing that holiness

---

[1] J. D. Denniston, *Greek Prose Style*, pp. 28–9.

[2] F. M. Cornford seems at one time to have thought this: see *From Religion to Philosophy*, pp. 249–61.

exists. As we may hold that some Greek gods were adulterous without supposing that there were any Greek gods, so we may hold that there are many virtues without supposing that there are any virtues. In ordinary language – ordinary ancient Greek as well as ordinary modern English – one may say that anything 'is' in some sense – εἶναι πως; but then, εἶναι πως is a far cry from εἶναι. It is one thing to be 'in a sense'; it is another to be an element in the real world. It is not unreasonable, then, to suppose that the commitment of ordinary language or common sense to the existence of, say, justice, is very much on a par with its commitment to Mr Pickwick. There was, of course, such a person as Mr Pickwick – he once journeyed with Sam Weller to Eatanswill for the elections. But Pickwickian journeys are like Pickwickian justice in that, though each in their own way is full of interest, they are ontologically dull. Why should this not also be true of the talk of Forms in the early dialogues?

The question is easily answered. There is no reason to suppose that the commitment of the early dialogues to the existence of Forms may be measured by the commitment to or tolerance of 'abstract entities' in ordinary Greek. Holiness, in the *Euthyphro*, is treated as a universal, standard, and essence. This treatment is technical and official; ordinary language is not committed to the existence of abstractions conceived in this way. It is true that Protagoras, in thinking that there is such a thing as justice, did not thereby conceive it as a Form; but then he did not know what justice is. It is true that Euthyphro early on accepts the suggestion that holiness is an ἰδέα; how little he understands it is shown by the dialectic of the remainder of the dialogue. The commitment to Forms in the early dialogues is not 'merely a matter of language'. It is a matter of metaphysics – a metaphysics of essence.

But if Socrates is armed with a theory in metaphysics, how is it that he is able to apply it – and indeed take it for granted – in conversation with ordinary men? The answer is that, though the theory of Forms is indeed a metaphysical theory, it is also essentially continuous with common sense, being, in one sense of that overworked word, a theory of meaning. 'What do you say temperance is?' Socrates asks Charmides. 'Since you know how to speak Greek, you no doubt can say what it seems to you to be.'[1]

---

[1] *Charmides*, 159a; cf. *Laches*, 197e, *Protagoras*, 329d, *Alcibiades*, I, 111c, 112a–d.

When Critias charges Socrates with arguing only to refute him, Socrates replies:[1]

> How can you believe, if I try my best to refute you, that I do so from any other motive than to examine what my own words mean, lest it should at some point escape my notice that I think I know something I do not.

Plain men had talked of holiness long before Socrates came to ask them what it was exactly that they meant. His inquiry was distinguished by the precision of it. He did not want synonyms of holiness, or examples of it, or distinguishing marks of it, but an analysis of the essence of it. His question is hardly one that common sense, left to its own devices, will ask. But it is a question to which common sense may surely be led, and the dialectic of the *Euthyphro* is in fact a record of such leading, as Socrates works throughout to make Euthyphro see the real nature of his question. The progress of dialectic involves passage from the respondent's naïve existence assumption that 'there is such a thing as holiness' to his acceptance, if dialectic is successful, of the highly sophisticated existence assumption that there is an essence of holiness, and that it can be defined. But if the latter claim is true, the passage is continuous: for a commitment to essence is then latent in our ordinary use of words. The essence of holiness is what the word 'holiness' means; to the degree that we do not understand that essence, we do not understand the meaning of our words.

Reducibility

The early dialogues are studded with assertions, stated or implied, that Forms exist; and those assertions are not to be dismissed as mere matters of language. But since the evidence for this has long been known to scholars who have yet rejected the conclusion, it may be well to pursue the issue further.

One might imagine an argument such as this. The text undoubtedly asserts that Forms exist; but it does not *need* that assertion. Talk about Forms in the early dialogues is avoidable, in that the putative ontological commitment found there is in fact a covert linguistic commitment after all. Plato – one might imagine the argument running – had an unfortunate though no doubt un-

[1] *Charmides*, 166c–d.

avoidable predilection for the material mode of speech, for representing as facts about the world items which are actually facts about language. Socratic dialectic is offered as an analysis of the nature of things; but that, after all, is an avoidable manner of speaking. Statements which assert or imply the existence of Forms are reducible to, or analysable without logical remainder into, statements which do not assert the existence of Forms. Questions about essence are, as even Plato himself would have agreed, questions about meaning, and questions about meaning are properly linguistic. Socratic dialectic, properly understood – and Plato no doubt did not properly understand it – is directed not toward the world but toward the meaning of words. Thus, to say that Forms exist is presumably to say that words are meaningful and that by inquiry we may hope to make their meaning clear. To say that Forms are universals is to say that there are words which have the same meaning in different contexts, and describe things to which we refer. To say that Forms are standards is to say that to understand the meaning of a description is to gain means to identify the circumstances in which it applies. To say that Forms are essences is to say that not every account of the meaning of a description correctly expresses what that meaning is. Socrates' question, 'What is the holy?', in short, reduces to the question, 'What does the word "holy" mean?' Therefore, the issue of whether there is an ontological commitment to Forms in the early dialogues is double, and admits a double answer. If the question is whether the text of those dialogues affirms the existence of Forms, the answer is Yes. If it is whether the logic of the position Plato is expounding requires the existence of Forms, the answer is No.

We are left to decide, then, whether Socrates' question, 'What is the holy?' can be reduced to the question, 'What does the word "holiness" mean?' It turns out that this substitution cannot, without circularity, be made.

Under some circumstances, the question, 'What does the word "holiness" mean?' might be lexicographical, a question to be answered by Prodicus or the dictionary. But plainly, Socrates in asking, 'What is the holy?' is not engaged in a search for verbal synonyms. Even Euthyphro does not suggest that Socrates should be satisfied with the answer that holiness is piety.

Again, the question, 'What does the word "holiness" mean?'

may be answered by an 'ostensive definition', an appeal to example. But whether example is construed narrowly, as a concrete instance, or more broadly as a general case exhibiting the character required, this sort of answer to the 'What is it?' question is rejected in the early dialogues wherever it occurs: Euthyphro cannot define holiness as 'just what I am doing now', or more generally, as prosecuting murderers and temple thieves.

Again, 'What does the word "holiness" mean?' may be answered by providing distinguishing marks of holiness, criteria of application or rules of use of the word 'holy'. But even if the notion of a distinguishing mark is taken in its strongest sense – *id quod omni et soli et semper*, a condition both necessary and sufficient for applying the term – this question is not equivalent to the question, 'What is the holy?', since the provision of a distinguishing mark or convertible criterion may leave the latter question unanswered. When Euthyphro defines the holy as what all the gods love, Socrates does not undertake to show that this mark fails to distinguish all and only those things which are holy; he implicitly grants this, or at least allows its possibility. Nor does he, as he might easily have done, question whether such a mark would be of any practical use in identifying instances of holiness. Rather, he argues that although Euthyphro may have happened on a πάθος of holiness, something which happens to be true of holy things, he has not shown the οὐσία of holiness, its nature and reality. The provision of a distinguishing mark, then, leaves the question, 'What is the holy?' unanswered.

But there is another sort of answer to the question, 'What does the word "holiness" mean?' It is a dull answer, but for present purposes, an important one. It is that the meaning of 'holiness' is holiness.

And what, pray, is holiness?

Precisely.

Questions about Forms in the early dialogues are not reducible to questions about the meaning of words, because the primary questions about the meaning of words reduce to questions about Forms. If irreducibility is to be the criterion of ontological commitment, there is an ontological commitment to Forms in the early dialogues.

The theory of meaning which gives rise to this commitment needs to be further explored. But the reader may well still be left with a lingering doubt. William James once remarked that imaginary fire is (not the kind of fire you can talk about avoidably but) the kind of fire that won't burn real sticks. This echoes Plato's own criterion of ontological commitment in the *Sophist* (247e), which he supposed was shared by Gods and Giants alike: it is that the mark of being is power, power to act or to be acted upon (πάθημα ἢ ποίημα ἐκ δυνάμεώς τινος, 248b). A difference, to be a difference, should make a difference. If Forms are to exist, we might expect them, not as it were to just sit there, but to do honest work, to affect the career of the world. This they do; for we shall find that, in the early dialogues, Forms are causes.

Essence and Reference

If the meaning of the word 'holiness' is holiness, and if holiness is a Form or essence, it is reasonable to suppose that the relation holding between the word and the thing is one of designation or naming. The early dialogues support this view. In the *Protagoras*, Socrates asks whether the thing (πρᾶγμα) which Protagoras has just named (ὠνομάσατε) is just or unjust (330c); and later, the question of whether virtue is one or many takes the form of an inquiry whether 'wisdom', 'justice', 'temperance', 'courage', and 'holiness' are names (ὀνόματα) for different things or names for the same thing.[1] The early dialogues assume a referential theory of meaning: they assume that abstract nouns, or some of them, are names.

'Meaning', Professor Quine has remarked, 'is what essence becomes when it is divorced from the object of reference and wedded to the word.'[2] By contrast, essence is what meaning becomes when it is divorced from the word and wedded to the object. What is meant then becomes, on occasion at least, not merely the sense of an expression, a bit of content more or less adequate to the economy of the world, but itself an item in the economy of the world whose nature is there for discovery. Because we understand the world imperfectly, we understand the meaning of our words, or some of them, imperfectly; put in another way, there is a difference between what we ordinarily mean by an expression, its overt or explicit content, and what we should mean if we understood

---

[1] *Protagoras*, 349b–c; cf. *Laches*, 198c, *Meno*, 74c, d, *Charmides*, 163d.
[2] *From a Logical Point of View*, p. 22.

the essence which that expression designates. Euthyphro is quite able to say what he ordinarily means by holiness; he means prosecuting murderers and temple thieves; on reflection, he means what is loved by the gods; on further reflection, what is loved by all the gods. But none of these states the essence of holiness. There is a difference between his grasp and his intention, between the account he is able to give of holiness and the essence he is attempting to explain. If to mean is sometimes to name, and what is named is an essence, then what is meant is often not a given, but a goal.

If meaning on occasion implies essence, and if our knowledge of essences is often defective, then it will not be true of ordinary language that 'everything is in order as it is', for the rules of use which govern words are not necessarily the rules by which they should be governed. The solution, it may be, is to deny essences:[1]

> One thinks that one is tracing the outline of the thing's nature over and over again, and one is merely tracing round the frame through which we look at it. A picture held us captive. And we could not get outside it, for it lay in our language and language seemed to repeat it to us inexorably. When philosophers use a word . . . and try to grasp the essence of the thing, one must ask oneself: is the word ever actually used this way in the language game which is its original home? — What *we* do is to bring words back from their metaphysical to their everyday use.

So Wittgenstein, who knew very well against what he was protesting. If this view is true, the assumptions on which Socratic dialectic rest are false. So are the typical Socratic claims about the unity of virtue: that virtue is knowledge, that courage is wisdom, that holiness is just. The words are not used that way every day — no more in ancient Greek than in modern English. Protagoras, in sopposing that a man could be courageous but not wise, was exhibiting the rules of use of his language. Socrates' connection of things which are linguistically distinct, unless it is to be dismissed as mere tyrannical legislation over language, is unintelligible apart from the notion of essence.

---

[1] Ludwig Wittgenstein, *Philosophical Investigations*, para. 114–16. The position directly under criticism is Wittgenstein's own in the *Tractatus*, but I suppose the comment to be relevant to the present context.

Essence and Ordinary Language

Socratic dialectic is not inquiry into the ordinary use of words, but inquiry into the characteristics in things which ground the use of words. The use of a word is no doubt connected with the characteristic it designates; if we are not always clear about the nature of things, it does not thereby follow that we stand in utter darkness. But the connection between essence and use is contingent: in a strict sense of the term 'criterion', the essence which a word designates is a criterion, and the only trustworthy criterion, for applying it.

There is an objection to this view.[1] We learned to talk at our mother's knee, and to know how to talk is to know how to use general terms; to know how to use general terms, however, is to be able to cite clear cases which other speakers of the language would certainly agree are examples of them. Knowing how to use a general term, of course, is different from being able to give a criterion for its use; but then, we are able to discover criteria by observing the use. Thus, we may often know perfectly well that a given action is holy without being able to cite a criterion for applying the word 'holy'; and furthermore, we may often better learn what it is to be holy by being given examples rather than a criterion. Socratic dialectic is therefore misconceived. It is mistaken in refusing to allow appeal to example in the search for meaning; it is in a parallel way mistaken in assuming that meaning must be fixed before examples can be determined. Due to these mistakes, Socratic dialectic is left in air, with no sound means of determining when a satisfactory criterion of meaning has been found, and this fact may well be taken to explain why the dialectic of the early dialogues so consistently ends in failure. The rules of the game have been so set that no one can win it.

There is, clearly, a point to this objection. Euthyphro cannot define holiness either by appeal to example or by appeal to what speakers of his language ordinarily understood by the term. How then can he define it at all? There is an obvious problem of knowledge here. As it happens, it is a problem which Plato stated as a paradox of inquiry in the *Meno*, and solved, as we shall see, by the doctrine of Recollection.

But if the problem of knowledge is obvious, it is also obviously

---

[1] For further discussion, see P. T. Geach, *Monist* 50 (1966), pp. 371–73.

a real one, for Socrates' assumption that what it is to be holy cannot be defined by offering examples of holiness is not merely correct, but obviously correct. If a is an example of F, and if for that reason we claim that a defines what it is to be F, then if b is an example of F, to be b is to be a; and since a defines what it is to be F, to be F is to be a. We may then say alternately that a is not an example of F, because it is what it is to be F, or that F is an example and the only example of itself. The source of the peculiarity here becomes evident if we substitute for 'F', whence it becomes clear that 'what it is to be holy' does duty, not for the adjective 'holy', but for the abstract noun 'holiness'. What would it mean to define holiness in terms of this or that thing being holy?

Parallel considerations hold for Socrates' claim that it is impossible to know that any given thing is holy without knowing the nature of holiness. The propositions 'I know that a is F' and 'I do not know what it is to be F' are incompatible. If I know that a is F, I know that a is an example of what it is to be F; if I do not know what it is to be F, I do not know what it is which a is an example of, and if I do not know what it is which a is an example of, I do not know that a is an example of F, and therefore do not know that a is F. It follows that what it is to be F is a criterion for determining whether a is F, since it is only through knowledge of the characteristic of which a is an example that one can determine that a is an example of that characteristic. So knowledge of what it is to be holy is prior to knowledge that any given thing is holy.

It may be urged that this defence of Socratic dialectic loads the dice. It turns on the related notions of definition and of knowing what something is – which is precisely the Socratic mistake. The appropriate aim of philosophical inquiry is not definition, but analysis of use. The kind of inquiry conducted in the *Euthyphro* is not such analysis, and because this is so, it is in some strict sense a (no doubt pious) fraud.

But the claim of fraudulence works two ways. Consider the issue with which the dialectic of the *Euthyphro* specifically attempts to deal: the resolution of conflict in moral judgement. It is suggested that we should arrive at criteria for the use of moral terms by appeal to example. Yet as a practical matter, the need for a criterion is felt precisely when examples diverge. Inconsistency of examples augurs inconsistency of criteria: if your criterion rules out my example, I may reject my example, but I may equally reject your criterion – much will depend, no doubt, on whose ox is gored. If the only appeal in moral argument is to criteria of use extracted from examples, Euthyphro and his father are each in a logically impregnable position. There is no final way of settling moral disputes except by recourse to Cromwellian kinds of discourse – to prove our doctrine orthodox by Apostolic blows and knocks.

But perhaps this prospect is unduly bleak. Moral disagreement, it may be claimed, arises only in boundary cases, and may be settled by appeal to clear examples. We speak blithely of the class of things which are F, visualizing it as a sort of objectified Venn diagram, with all the Fs neatly placed within and all the non-Fs without a precisely described circle. The truth is that most general terms in ordinary language, as distinct from mathematics, carry with them a penumbra in which the conditions of their application are unclear: example shades into example in such a way that between what is clearly F and what is clearly not F there is a range, a quasi-continuum, in which it is difficult to know what to say. This is a cup, and that a bowl, but here is something you may call either or neither or both. Still, we may look to clear cases to adjudicate the doubtful ones, and anyone who does not recognize clear cases for what they are does not understand the language in which he is discussing them. If you do not think that this from which I now drink my coffee is a cup, you do not know what the word 'cup' means. So, too, by parity, with moral terms.

It would be pleasant if this were true. Unfortunately, it is not. Moral terms, as Plato once remarked, 'have no image wrought visibly to men.'[1] However it may be with empirical terms, issues of good and evil, right and wrong, have the peculiarity that one man's clear case is penumbral for a second and umbral for a third, and this in regard not merely to the periphery but to the most central issues with which moral reasoning has to deal. It is perhaps unnecessary – mercifully – to argue this point by citing examples; in this cruel and troubled century, the reader may be left to provide his own. But one may perhaps venture to remark that, while it may or may not be a paradox that virtue is knowledge, it is merely preposterous to suppose that vice is aphasia. If questions of good and evil are not questions about the games people play with

---

[1] *Politicus* 286c, cf. 277d, *Phaedrus* 250a–b.

language, or about attitudes or customs or tastes, if there is or may be such a thing as moral knowledge, then the *Euthyphro*'s claim that knowledge consists in the discernment of essence, while it may be false, is assuredly not fraudulent. It would be unwise to reject it without facing squarely the problems with which it is meant to deal.

Unum Nomen Unum Nominatum

Referential theories of meaning have often been thought to carry a peculiar corollary, *unum nomen unum nominatum*, and a variety of critics have thought they detected this assumption in the early dialogues. Mr Richard Robinson has said that 'If Socrates' question (What is X?) is to be a legitimate question admitting of an answer . . . we must assume that the word X is univocal'.[1] Professor Ross also finds this implication in the Socratic question, and infers that 'Plato was alive to the possibility of ambiguity in the meaning of a name. But apparently he regarded this as occurring somewhat rarely, and was not fully alive to the varying shades of meaning which even the most seemingly innocent name may have.'[2] But this rests on mistaken inference. Socrates assumes that one can ask and answer such questions as 'What is holiness?'; he further assumes that holiness is a Form or essence; but these assumptions have no bearing on the question of whether words such as 'holy' and 'holiness' are or may be used in different senses. That false inference disguises a dull truth, which is that Socrates assumes that holiness is an essence in order to explain, among other things, how it is that we call different things by the same name and mean the same thing by so calling them. This in no way implies *unum nomen unum nominatum*, if that is supposed to mean, as a claim about ordinary language, that for each word there is one and only one correct meaning, and that ambiguity is impossible.[3]

Nor does it imply, as Professor Ross and Mr Robinson presuppose, a rigid disjunction between univocity and equivocity. We are prone to suppose that sameness in meaning and difference in meaning are exclusive and exhaustive alternatives. If meaning

---

[1] *PED*, p. 58. Mr Robinson cites *Meno*, 74d, and *Republic*, X, 596a, to support this claim. See also *Republic*, II, 368e–369b, IV, 435a–b.

[2] *PTI*, p. 12.

[3] For Plato's explicit awareness of ambiguity, see *Euthydemus*, 277d–278b, 295c 299d.

is reference, the result is a sharp-edged theory of universals, a theory in which each significant word either introduces the same universal in exactly the same way, or introduces a different universal. But this neglects the fact that meanings may differ and yet be organized around a common nucleus in an order of priority and posteriority. Thus, for example, men are just and actions are just. But Socrates in the *Republic* (IV, 443e–444a) argues that just actions are those which preserve or help produce justice as a condition of soul in men; it follows that the meaning of the word 'just' as applied to an action must be defined in terms of its meaning as applied to a man. The adjective, then, is used in a primary sense of men, and in a derivative sense of actions, and this is neither univocity nor equivocity, but eponymy.[1] But it is the same Form which is introduced both in primary and derivative uses; it is merely introduced in different ways. This is not to suggest that Plato recognized the fact of eponymy in the early dialogues, though, in point of fact, there is strong indication that this is so.[2] It is to suggest, however, that there is no incompatibility between the theory of Forms and the eponymous use of terms. And, as we shall see, in the middle dialogues Forms themselves become the primary designata of certain kinds of eponyms.

If the tag *unum nomen unum nominatum* is to be applied at all to the early dialogues, it should not be understood as a claim about ordinary language, nor as excluding eponymy. It is best taken as an ideal for the improvement of language, a demand that the texture of a vocabulary match the economy of the world. In the *Cratylus*, a name is said to be an instrument analogous to a shuttle. One weaves with a shuttle, separating warp and woof; just so, one teaches with a name, separating things according to what they are (388b–c). And as the shuttle is made, not just by anyone, but by a

---

[1] For further discussion, see J. L. Austin, *Philosophical Papers*, pp. 39–42; Joseph Owens, *The Doctrine of Being in the Aristotelian Metaphysics* (2nd ed.), pp. 107–35; G. E. L. Owen, *Aristotle and Plato in the Mid-Fourth Century* (ed. Owen and Düring), pp. 163–90. Names for eponymy have varied. Austin called it 'paronymy', which, in view of *Categories*, 1a, 12 ff., is infelicitous. Father Owens calls it 'equivocity by reference', which shades possible areas of disagreement over logical and metaphysical uses. Professor Owen calls it 'focal meaning', which suggests an analogy which is misleading, since it is not the concentration by refraction of what had previously been diffuse. The word 'eponymy' is neutral, and derived from Plato's own use.

[2] See *Lysis*, 220a–b, 219c–d.

carpenter, who looks to the Form of the shuttle itself rather than to any model which can be made and broken, so too names should be given, not just by anyone, but by a Name-maker, 'who is of all craftsmen the rarest' (389a); the Name-maker will look to the Form of the name itself in giving names, fitting each name to its proper use (389d), and as the weaver judges the worth of the work of the carpenter, so the dialectician will judge the worth of the work of the giver of names (390c). Platonism, in its attitude toward ordinary language, is inherently revisionary.

This enterprise of giving names is committed to *unum nomen unum nominatum*, however, in a sense other than any yet indicated. In the *Meno* (71e ff.), when Meno is asked to define virtue, he replies with a list of virtues, each of which has its own definition: the virtue of a man is to manage his city, benefit friends, and harm enemies; the virtue of a woman is to order her household and obey her husband; and there are other virtues for children, slaves, and the elderly. Socrates rejects this answer: Meno has given him a swarm of virtues, whereas he had asked for an account of that one thing, virtue, which is the same in them all.[1] This, of course, assumes that there *is* one thing, that in addition to 'virtue of *x*' and 'virtue of *y*' and so on, there is 'virtue', which is common to the various 'virtues of'. Put otherwise, 'virtue' is not a blanket-word, nor an incomplete expression: it is the name of an essence. This could be taken to explain why, when we speak of a man's virtue and a woman's virtue, we are neither using eponyms nor simply equivocating; but in both the *Meno* and the *Theaetetus* it is rather taken to indicate a higher and more interesting level of generality. The Name-maker who knows his business will presumably bear it in mind.

Essential Causality

Forms, to borrow a phrase from Locke, are real and not nominal essences. They are real because they cannot be made nominal: inquiry into them is not inquiry into names or the ordinary meanings of words, except as inquiry into names or the ordinary meanings of words is inquiry into them. But they are also real because they are what real things are. As Locke put it:[2]

---

[1] See also *Theaetetus*, 146c–147c, which makes a parallel point about defining knowledge, and *Sophist*, 257c–d.

[2] *Essay*, II, iii, 15.

Essence may be taken for the being of anything whereby it is what it is. And thus the real internal, but generally in substances unknown, constitution of things, whereon their discoverable qualities depend, may be called their essence. This is the proper signification of the word, as is evident from the formation of it; *essentia*, in its primary notation, signifying properly being.

By Locke's account, an essence is 'the being of anything whereby it is what it is'. Aristotle in the *Metaphysics* made this claim, identifying the substantial form of an individual with its substance, essence with the being of that which has the essence. He thus founded the tradition Locke inherited.

But in Plato's early dialogues Forms are not the being of that of which they are Forms. A universal, being one, cannot constitute the being of a plurality – precisely why Aristotle was led to distinguish substantial form from universal.[1] The *Euthyphro* does not imply that holiness is the being of any given holy thing or action as holy; it implies only that holiness is that *by* which holy things are holy. It implies, to borrow another bit of Aristotelian vocabulary, that holiness is a cause.

There is an argument in the *Hippias Major* which makes this assumption explicit. Socrates leads Hippias to agree that justice *is* something (ἔστι τι τοῦτο), and that this is true of wisdom too, for, 'things which are just and wise and so on would not be such *by* them, if they were not something'. Because beautiful things are beautiful by beauty, Hippias is compelled to agree that beauty *is* something too. Socrates then goes on to raise the question: What is it? (*Hippias Major*, 287c–d).

The argument is an excellent one: if beauty is that by which beautiful things are beautiful, and if beautiful things exist, beauty exists. Beauty is not a word, not a thought, not a concept. It is an existing thing, for the things it makes beautiful are existing things, and they are not made beautiful by our words or thoughts or concepts.

This argument is put explicitly only in the *Hippias Major*, but it is assumed by every early dialogue which aims at definition, for the assumption that Forms are essences is essential to dialectic: Forms are universals and standards precisely because they are that by which things are that they are.

[1] Cf. *Metaphysics*, VII, xiii, xiv.

It is because Forms are essences that Plato so often uses causal language to characterize their relation with the things which have them. In the *Lysis* (221c) Socrates remarks that 'When a cause is destroyed, it is surely impossible for that of which it is the cause to continue to exist.' Holiness is in this sense a cause: its existence is necessary to the existence of holy things in so far as they are holy.

The early dialogues use a variety of metaphors to describe the relation between Forms and their instances. Forms are said to be 'in' their instances, or 'present to' them, or to be 'added' to them, or to be 'at' them. The instances, on the other hand, 'have' them or 'accept' them or 'get' them or 'have a share' of them.[1] All of these metaphors are found in ordinary language.[2] They may be used quite normally with abstract nouns in Greek, just as in English one may say that there is courage in an action, or that the presence of justice would improve a situation, or that one man has a greater measure of patience than another.

As metaphors, and as familiar Greek, these terms provided material for sophistic quibbles. In the *Euthydemus*, for example, Dionysodorus asks whether a beautiful thing is other than the beautiful. When Socrates, after hesitating for a moment, replies that beautiful things are other than beauty itself (αὐτὸ τὸ καλόν), but that each of them has a certain beauty (κάλλος τι) present to it, Dionysodorus is quick to grasp the handle. 'Then if an ox comes to be present to you,' he says, 'you are an ox. And since I am present, you are Dionysodorus' (301a). 'Heaven forbid,' says Socrates, and with reason. But the question is not trivial: 'presence' is a metaphor – or at least a word with many uses – and a good deal turns on its meaning.

The presence in question is of a peculiar kind. In the *Lysis* Socrates undertakes to explain how evil may be present to what is neither good nor evil, and breaks off his discussion to clarify his meaning. 'Some things,' he says, 'are such as to be themselves such as that which is present to them; others are not.'[3] If, for example, blond hair is painted white, whiteness will be present to the hair, but the hair will not itself be white. But when in age the hair turns white, whiteness will be present to it in a different sense,

---

[1] For a representative though incomplete selection of passages, see *PTI*, pp. 228–9.

[2] And are not therefore in the strict sense metaphorical.

[3] *Lysis*, 217c, trans. A. E. Taylor.

for the hair will then be white. In the former case, whiteness is present to the hair. In the latter, the hair is 'white by the presence of whiteness'.

To explain the special sense in which whiteness is present to a thing when it is white, Socrates has recourse to the instrumental dative. This device occurs frequently in the early dialogues. Holy things are holy *by* holiness, temperate men temperate *by* temperance,[1] beautiful things beautiful *by* beauty.[2] Beauty, according to the *Hippias Major* (300a), *makes* (ποιεῖν) beautiful things beautiful. These expressions are tied to ordinary usage. Ion thinks that it is *by* knowledge (instrumental dative) that he can praise Homer (*Ion*, 541e). Socrates thinks we are benefited *by* (ὑπό and the genitive of agent) health (*Crito*, 47d). Wisdom *makes* men fortunate (*Euthydemus*, 280a). Temperance is good if it *makes* those to whom it is present good, but not bad (*Charmides* 161a).

But though these expressions are tied to ordinary language, they are often used by Socrates in an unordinary way. Ποιεῖν is the regular active of πάσχειν, and πάσχειν may regularly mean 'to be qualified'; but ποιεῖν is not regularly used in the sense of 'to qualify'. Furthermore, there is a considerable logical difference between saying that wisdom makes men fortunate, and that wisdom makes men wise, or is that by which they are wise.[3]

These expressions are causal – causal not in the sense commonly associated with the banging of billiard balls, but in a sense analogous to that in which Aristotle speaks of a formal cause. Beauty is a cause of beautiful things in precisely this sense: its existence is a necessary condition for the existence of other things in so far as they are beautiful.[4] It is for that reason that, in the *Hippias Major*, Socrates claims that the things people call beautiful *are* beautiful only if beauty itself exists, and that since Hippias has defined beauty as a beautiful maiden, something exists by reason of which (δι' ὅ) beautiful things are beautiful.[5]

Forms are causes, then, in the sense that they are essences by which things are what they are. So it is that, in the *Phaedo* (100c),

---

[1] *Protagoras*, 332b. See also the parallel use of ὑπό and the genitive of **agent, 332e.**
[2] *Hippias Major*, 287c–d.
[3] A sign of this is that 'Wisdom makes men fortunate' may be read in extension: 'Whoever is wise has good fortune'. But this will not do for 'Wisdom makes men wise', which surely does not mean 'Whoever is wise is wise'.
[4] Cf. *Lysis*, 221c, quoted above.
[5] 288a; cf. *Meno*, 72c.

Socrates suggests that beautiful things are beautiful 'for no other reason than because' they partake of beauty, and asks Cebes if he accepts this kind of cause (αἰτία). F. M. Cornford explained this passage as follows:[1]

> The phrase 'for no other reason than because' . . . is ambiguous. 'Reason' might mean 'explanation' (a common use of αἰτία). The premise will then assert that the statement 'This rose is beautiful' is equivalent to 'This rose partakes of Beauty': I can substitute that form of words and so explain the sense by paraphrase. But Plato seems to be speaking, not of the analysis of a statement, but of the corresponding fact. The theory will then assert that this fact consists of (1) a particular visible thing, this rose; (2) the Form, Beautiful or Beauty; and (3) what we should call a relation between the two expressed by 'is', for which we can substitute 'partakes of'. But once more we have, so far, only an explanation: the fact that this rose is beautiful is the same thing as the fact that this rose partakes of Beauty. We learn nothing about any *cause* which would bring that fact into existence. On either view we have only an analysis of a statement or of a fact, not a reason for the statement being true or a cause of the fact's existence.

The first suggestion may be ruled out. You can only explain a statement by paraphrase to someone ignorant of what the original words mean, and no one who failed to understand 'This rose is beautiful' would find it illuminating to be told that the expression means 'This rose partakes of Beauty'. Nor is there any ancient evidence to show that αἰτία could be used of a paraphrase. The suggestion that 'for no other reason than because' may imply paraphrase, then, is insufficient.

There remains what Cornford calls 'the analysis of the corresponding fact'. But if the fact that this rose is beautiful is the same fact as the fact that this rose partakes of beauty, it is not clear, as he recognizes, in what way analysis differs from paraphrase. In any case, this misses Plato's point. 'This rose is beautiful' and 'This rose partakes of the Form of Beauty' are indeed equivalent statements – if the theory of Forms is true. But that theory is precisely a theory of ontological priority in the structure of facts, not a theory of statement equivalences[2]. The *presence* of the Form

[1] *PP*, pp. 76-7.

[2] See A. E. Taylor, *Commentary on Plato's Timaeus*, p. 342, on *Timaeus*, 52a, 5, and *ACPA*, p. 178, n. 102.

of beauty is a necessary and sufficient condition for calling this rose beautiful: we baptize the thing because of the character in it, and the *presence* of that character (as distinct from the character itself) ensures the appropriateness of the baptism. The Form itself, however, is only a necessary condition for the beauty of the rose: it is a cause of that beauty in that if it did not exist the rose would not exist as beautiful. The Form, as distinct from the *presence* of the Form, is not a sufficient condition for the beauty of the rose, for it is not a sufficient condition for its own presence in the rose: that depends, not only on the existence of beauty, but on the condition of the soil, and the climate, and the skill of the gardener. Sufficiency of condition here involves efficient causality, not merely essential causality.[1]

Forms, then, are causes in the sense that they are that by which things are what they are. They therefore affect the career of the world, in that if they did not exist, the world would not be what it is. This then, is the basis of the ontological commitment to the existence of Forms in the early dialogues.

Reference Revisited

The early dialogues assume a referential theory of meaning, in the sense that abstract nouns, or some of them, name objects. It does not follow from this that the early dialogues assume the thesis, now less widely held than formerly, that to describe something involves naming a description. This last thesis has generally been connected with a further one: that the structure of well-formed (or well-analysed) sentences must stand in one-to-one or biunique

---

[1] At *Phaedo*, 100d, Socrates claims that the presence of beauty *makes* things beautiful. Cornford (p. 77) remarks: 'But again the word "makes" is ambiguous. Does it mean that the thing's beauty simply *consists in* the presence either of the Form itself or of the character like that of the Form, as we say the presence of a gay colour "makes" the thing gay? Or does it mean that the Form, existing independently, *causes* the thing to be (or to become) beautiful by somehow imparting its own character to the thing? This is precisely the dilemma on which Socrates refuses to pronounce. The language might be expressly designed to leave it unsolved.'

But the dilemma is factitious. It depends on the contrast between consisting in and causing. But if causing means efficient causality, there is a contrast, but no dilemma, since this is not what Socrates means by 'makes'. If on the other hand causing means essential causality, there is no contrast between consisting in and causing, and no dilemma: if the beauty of the rose consists in the presence of beauty in it, then Beauty is a cause of the presence of beauty in the rose, in that if Beauty did not exist there would be no beauty in the rose; so consisting in presupposes causing.

correspondence to the facts those sentences represent. Since well-formed sentences contain predicates, the facts they represent must contain predicate-analogues; it is but a step further to suppose that those predicate analogues are universals or essences, and that predicates name them.

This is a thesis which Plato did not hold. The early dialogues, indeed, can hardly be said to bear on it; their concern is with the question of what certain things are, not with the question of how and in what way things may be said of things. But if we look to the *Phaedo*, we find that describing something appears to involve, not naming a description, but naming the thing described. For, 'Each of the Forms exists, and the other things, because they come to have a share of them, are named after them'.[1] This strongly suggests that to describe Socrates as just is to name him just, and not to name justice at all; though the name, if applied truly, applies because Socrates partakes of justice.

The relation between 'just' and 'justice' is an example of what Aristotle, using what may well have been an Academic distinction, called paronymy: 'When things get their name from something, with a difference in ending, they are called *paronymous*. Thus, for example, the grammarian gets his name from grammar, the brave get theirs from bravery.'[2] So in naming Socrates just we name him paronymously: he gets his name from justice, with difference in ending. But since the name of the Form in which Socrates partakes need not differ in grammatical ending from the name Socrates gets from it, it is perhaps better to follow Plato's own use and say that Socrates is named eponymously. If the theory of Forms is true, then 'Socrates is just' and 'Socrates partakes of justice' are equivalent statements; each implies the other. But the first contains two names for the same thing, one of which is an eponym, while the other contains two names for two things, neither of which is an eponym. In both cases, meaning involves reference; the objects of reference, however, are distinct, though eponymy is grounded in their connection.

It is a consequence of this view that species and genera are primary, while the descriptions which eponymously introduce them are derivative: the brave are named from bravery, not vice versa. But why, after all, should this be so? Why should we not

---

[1] *Phaedo*, 102b; cf. *Parmenides*, 130e. For further discussion, see *SPM*, pp. 45–7.
[2] *Categories*, 1a, 12 ff., trans. Ackrill.

regard species and genera as logical (or, mayhap, illogical) constructions, the primary vehicle of meaning being descriptions themselves? Plato's main answer to this in the middle dialogues would have been the One over Many argument,[1] the premisses of which have been admirably stated, in modern dress, by John Austin – who did not, of course, subscribe to its conclusion:[2]

> If there is to be communication of the sort that we achieve by language at all, there must be a stock of symbols of some kind which a communicator ('the speaker') can produce 'at will' and which a communicatee ('the audience') can observe: these may be called the 'words', though, of course, they need not be anything like what we should normally call words – they might be signal flags, &c. There must also be something other than the words, which the words are to be used to communicate about: this may be called the 'world'. There is no reason why the world should not contain the words, in every sense except the sense of the actual statement itself which on any particular occasion is being made about the world. Further, the world must exhibit (we must observe) similarities and dissimilarities (there could not be the one without the other): if everything were either absolutely indistinguishable from anything else or completely unlike anything else, there would be nothing to say. And finally (for present purposes – of course, there are other conditions to be satisfied too) there must be two sets of conventions: *Descriptive* conventions correlating the words (= sentences) with *types* of situation, thing, event, &c., to be found in the world. *Demonstrative* conventions correlating the words (= statements) with the *historic* situations, &c., to be found in the world.

Austin is generally called an Ordinary Language philosopher; but he marched under no banners and beat no drums, and the paragraph above, describing how the world must be if language is to be about it, is, if I mistake not, a piece of purest metaphysics. Austin goes on to add in a note:[3]

> 'Is of a type with which' means 'is sufficiently like those standard states of affairs with which'. Thus, for a statement to be true one state of affairs must be like certain others, which is a natural relation, but also *sufficiently* like to merit the same 'description', which

---

[1] Cf. *Parmenides*, 132a, 1–4.
[2] *Philosophical Papers*, pp. 89–90. Italics Austin's.
[3] *Ibid.*, p. 90, n. 2.

is no longer a purely natural relation. To say 'This is red' is not the same as to say 'This is like those', nor even to say 'This is like those which are called red'. That things are *similar*, or even 'exactly' similar, I may literally see, but that they are the *same* I cannot literally see – in calling them the same colour a convention is involved additional to the conventional choice of the name to be given to the colour they are said to be.

Perhaps. But then similarity and dissimilarity are relations which obtain in different respects. A cricket ball and a baseball are similar in shape and dissimilar in colour; we cannot merely state that they are similar and dissimilar without distinguishing the respects in which this is so.[1] If then we grant that similarity and dissimilarity are natural relations, obtaining between things in the world independently of the way we talk or the fact that we talk at all, it hardly seems plausible to suppose that the characteristics in virtue of which those relations obtain – shape characteristics, colour characteristics, and so on – are matters of linguistic convention.[2] If the relations are 'natural', it would appear that the characteristics in virtue of which they hold are equally so. Those characteristics, be it noted, are not descriptions: we say that the cricket ball and the baseball are both spherical, but we do not say that they resemble each other in respect of spherical, but in respect of *being* spherical, or sphericity. We describe the thing; but the description holds in virtue of the character of the thing described. This, I take it, is a reason for saying that the brave are named from bravery, rather than the reverse.

These remarks, of course, do not settle the issue between those who, finding a world of similarities and dissimilarities, infer the existence of characteristics, and those who, finding the same

[1] Though, of course, there may be kinds of similarity or resemblance, as, for example, the resemblance between cartoon and cartooned, in which we should not wish to say that the relation holds in virtue of the presence of common characteristics.

[2] Austin's objection that we do not *see* sameness of character, while we *do* see similarity, is puzzling. I should have thought that to see the similarity between a cricket ball and a baseball is precisely to see the respects (some of them) in which they are similar. Again, if I may see ('literally'?) that two things are similar, may I not also see that they have the same shape, and further, see that that shape is (say) spherical? I do not of course thereby see sphericity; but then I do not (in that sense) see similarity either. In general, it is hard to understand how linguistic convention can infect description *per se*, and yet leave natural similarity in health.

world, refuse the inference. But perhaps they do something to show the grounds on which, in Plato's case at least, the inference rested. It should be noted, however, that neither in the early nor in the middle dialogues is our knowledge of Forms derived from recognition of similarities; for it is only through the use of the Form as a standard that we may be assured that similarity in fact obtains.[1]

4. ONTOLOGICAL STATUS AND THE DEVELOPMENT OF THE THEORY OF FORMS

If Forms are to exist, it is reasonable to ask how they exist, or what their ontological status is. In the middle dialogues, notably the *Phaedo* and *Republic*, the relation between Forms and their instances is construed as one of radical dependence and radical separation: a New World has been discovered, whose contents are Forms unvexed by time, and that world is made the foundation of everything which is, standing to the world of sensible appearances as the more real to the less, as originals stand to shadows and reflections. Professor Cherniss has summed up the ontology of the middle dialogues admirably:[2]

> The phenomenal world, which as a whole and in all its parts is continuously in process, cannot be the reality which is the object of knowledge. The apparently disparate phenomena of human conduct, of mental activity, and of physical process can each and all be accounted for only on the assumption that there exist outside of the phenomenal process real entities which are the standards of conduct, the termini of process, and the objective correlates of knowledge. These entities are the ideas. . . .

This account describes what Professor Cherniss has elsewhere called the philosophical economy of the theory of Ideas;[3] that theory is a single key to many doors, a solution at once to problems in ethics, metaphysics, and epistemology.

The existence of this theory in the middle dialogues has cast its shadow backwards. It has led students who find a theory of Forms in the early dialogues to find this theory there. It has led students

---

[1] See *Phaedo*, 74d–75a.
[2] *REA*, p. 5.
[3] See *SPM*, ch. i.

who fail to find this theory in the early dialogues to deny that there is any theory there.

Three main views have been maintained. One is that the early and the middle dialogues are here the same: in both, Forms exist and are separate from the things which have them; there is a theory of Forms in the *Euthyphro*, and it is essentially the same theory propounded in the *Phaedo* and *Republic*, and later criticized in the *Parmenides*. A second view is that, though there are Forms in the early dialogues, they are not separate, being 'in' things and not 'apart' from them. A third view is that though the language of Forms is found in the early dialogues, Forms themselves are not: the theory propounded in the *Phaedo* and *Republic*, and criticized in the *Parmenides*, is wholly new, and Plato had invented no part of it – except its vocabulary – when he wrote the *Euthyphro*.

There is also a fourth view, which for present purposes may be treated as a variant of the third. It is that, in both the early and the middle dialogues, what have been called Forms are merely linguistic predicates, not independent universals or essences, so that the *Euthyphro* agrees with the *Phaedo* and *Republic* in respect to what it does not propound. What it is the existence of which the *Parmenides* does not criticize is left unstated.

The claim that there is no commitment to the existence of Forms in the early dialogues is mistaken, and may be dismissed without further discussion.[1] It remains to ask whether Forms in the early dialogues are 'in' things or 'separate' from them, 'immanent' or 'transcendent'. On this question the evidence of Aristotle has often been thought decisive, though examination will show that it is not.

Aristotle on Separation

Aristotle in the *Metaphysics* distinguishes Plato's thought from that of Socrates in the following way:[2]

> Socrates ... was busying himself about ethical matters and neglecting the world of nature as a whole, but seeking the universal in these ethical matters, and fixed thought for the first time on definitions; Plato accepted his teaching, but held that the problem applied not to sensible things but to entities of another kind –

[1] See above, pp. 105ff., Sec. III.
[2] *Metaphysics*, I, 987b, 1 ff., trans. Ross.

for this reason, that the common definition could not be a definition of any sensible thing, as they were always changing. Things of this other sort, then, he called Ideas, and sensible things, he said, were all named after these, and in virtue of a relation to these; for the many existed by participation in the Ideas that have the same name as they.

The point is later put in a different way:[1]

But when Socrates was occupying himself with the excellences of character, and in connexion with them became the first to raise the problem of universal definition . . . [he] did not make the universals or the definitions exist apart; they, however [the Platonists], gave them separate existence, and this was the kind of thing they called Ideas.

And again:[2]

They [The Platonists] thought that the particulars in the sensible world were in a state of flux and none of them remained, but that the universal was apart from these and something different. And Socrates gave the impulse to this theory, as we said in our earlier discussion, by reason of his definitions, but he did not *separate* universals from individuals; and in this he thought rightly, in not separating them. This is plain from the results; for without the universal it is not possible to get knowledge, but the separation is the cause of the objections that arise with regard to the Ideas. His successors, however, treating it as necessary, if there are to be any substances besides the sensible and transient substances, that they must be separable, had no others, but gave separate existence to these universally predicated substances, so that it followed that universals and individuals were almost the same sort of thing.

What does Aristotle mean by saying that the Ideas were χωριστά, 'separate'? He means, first of all, that they were separate as being numerically distinct from their instances – that is, as being themselves individual and one in number: the Platonists, 'at the same time make Ideas universal, and again treat them as separable and as individuals'.[3] This is an important premise in Aristotle's criticism of the theory of Forms, for Aristotle supposed that a universal cannot be individual, that what is predicated of many

[1] *Metaphysics*, XIII, 1078b, 18 ff.
[2] *Metaphysics*, XIII, 1086b, 2 ff.
[3] *Metaphysics*, XIII, 1086e, 33; cf. *Parmenides*, 129e–130b, and *Republic*, V, 475e–476a.

things cannot itself be one thing among many: 'Things that are individual and numerically one are, without exception, not said of any subject.'[1]

Numerical distinctness, however, is a necessary but not a sufficient condition for separation. At *Categories*, 1a, 24–25, Aristotle remarks that 'By "in a subject" I mean what is in something, not as a part, and cannot exist separately (χωρίς) from what it is in'. This text, along with Aristotle's subsequent remark that 'Nothing prevents [what is individual and one in number] from being present in a subject' (1b 7–8), suggests that separation implies existential independence as well as numerical distinctness. This independence must be construed as distributive, not collective; for by 'in a subject' Aristotle means, not merely 'cannot exist apart from some subject', but 'cannot exist apart from the particular subject it is in'.[2] In claiming that the Ideas are separate, then, Aristotle means that they are individuals, and that they exist independently of any given instances.[3] Since the existence of the Idea is a condition for the existence of its instances, separation, so defined, involves an asymmetrical relationship, that of ontological priority:[4]

> Some things are called prior and posterior . . . in respect of nature and substance, i.e. those which can be without other things, while

---

[1] *Categories*, 1b, 6–7, trans. Ackrill.

[2] See. J. L. Ackrill, *Aristotle's Categories and De Interpretatione*, pp. 73–4. Professor Owen has recently questioned this interpretation (*Phronesis*, X (1965, pp. 97–105), but at the cost of collapsing the distinction between presence and predicability which 1a, 24–5, is meant to help explain; it is as true of what is said of a subject as it is of what is in a subject that it cannot exist apart from *some* subject. What is not true is that it cannot exist apart from *this* subject.

[3] Thus W. F. R. Hardie's claim (*A Study in Plato*, p. 73) that 'To say that a form is "separate" is to say that there can be a form without there being particulars to exemplify it' is a mistaken account of Aristotle's meaning. It further mistakes Plato, since the evidence cited to show that this was Plato's view is drawn, not from texts implying lack of exemplification, but deficiency of exemplification. Plato may well have thought, as a matter of economy in the universe, that the existence of a Form implies the existence of instances of it, that Forms, so to speak, have existential import; this is, of course, a far cry from saying that the existence of a Form implies that this or that shall be an instance of it. *Republic*, V, 471c–472e, (cf. IX, 592a–b), has been cited as evidence for empty essences; it is in fact evidence that essences such as justice are only deficiently realized. See also Aristotle, *Posterior Analytics*, II, 92, b3–12, *Metaphysics*, VII, 1031a, 12 ff.

[4] *Metaphysics*, V, 1019a, 1 ff.

the others cannot be without them – a distinction which Plato first used.

By claiming that Plato separated the Ideas, then, Aristotle means that the Ideas are numerically distinct from their instances, exist independently of their instances, and are ontologically prior to their instances.[1] It was to this that Aristotle opposed his own theory of τὸ εἶδος τὸ ἔνον, the theory that the form of a materiate substance is neither numerically distinct from nor independent of that of which it is the form.

Socrates and Separation

In claiming that Plato separated the Ideas, Aristotle was surely correct.[2] But what did he understand by claiming that Socrates did *not* separate them? This must mean either that Socrates did not distinguish them from their instances, or that he did not regard them as independent of or prior to their instances.

Whether this is true of the historical Socrates is not here in question; with the evidence at our disposal, the issue is hardly decidable. But Aristotle's knowledge of the historical Socrates was presumably drawn mainly from Plato's portrait in the early dialogues, and for that reason his claim that Socrates did not separate the Ideas has often been treated as an interpretation of the early dialogues.[3] If, then, we are permitted to identify the historical Socrates with the early Platonic Socrates, the question is whether this interpretation of the early dialogues is accurate.

There is good reason to think that Aristotle, in denying that Socrates separated the Ideas, meant that Socrates did not distinguish Forms from their instances at all. For, after mentioning Socrates' search for definitions in *Metaphysics*, I, Aristotle goes on

---

[1] This account ignores another which has gained some currency in the literature. Julius Stenzel (*Zahl und Gestalt bei Platon und Aristotles*, pp. 133 ff.), held that Aristotle, in criticising separation, was not criticising Plato's account of the relation of particulars to Ideas, but his account of the relation of genera to *infimae species*, and specifically the view that genera in some way exist apart from species, that there may be a γένος παρὰ τὰ εἴδη. This thesis, approved by Taylor (*Plato*, p. 515), was questioned by Hardie (*A Study in Plato*, p. 74), and refuted by Cherniss, *ACPA*, n. 122.

[2] For a review of ancient evidence for separation, drawn from Plato and the testimony of Xenocrates as well as Aristotle, see *ACPA*, pp. 203–11 and nn. 121–5.

[3] See A. E. Taylor, *Varia Socratica*, pp. 40–1; for further discussion, see W. D. Ross, *Aristotle's Metaphysics*, vol. i, pp. xxxv–ix.

to add that 'Plato accepted his teaching, but held that the problem applied not to sensible things but to entities of another kind – for this reason, that the common definition could not be a definition of any sensible thing, as they were always changing'.[1] This implies that Socrates identified the objects of definition with sensibles, which is another way of saying that he did not distinguish Forms from their instances.[2]

But Socrates is plainly not defining sensibles in the early dialogues: quite apart from the fact that moral Forms have no sensible instances, the non-identity of Forms and their instances is assumed by the dialectic of every early dialogue which aims at definition, for definition is, as we have seen, an account of an object, and that object is a universal. Non-identity is also implied by the fact that Forms are essences and causes, by which things are what they are, and by the fact that Forms are standards for determining what things have them and what things do not. Nor is non-identity only a tacit assumption: at *Euthydemus*, 300e–301a, it is stated as a fact. When Dionysodorus there asks Socrates whether beautiful things are the same as or different from the beautiful, Socrates replies that, although there is a certain beauty present to them, they are different from the beautiful itself.

Perhaps, then, Aristotle should be understood, not as denying that Socrates distinguished Forms from their instances, but as allowing this and denying that their distinction was numerical, that Forms were individuals in their own right. There is, however, no textual evidence that this was Aristotle's view, and it is difficult to suppose that he could have held it. It implies that Socrates had attained to that notion of non-individualized form which Aristotle knew to be his own: the notion that form is a thing which is, but which is neither individual nor one in number. It is, of course, a paradox to suggest that a thing can be and yet not be one in number, and Aristotle himself was led to embrace that paradox only as a result of long reflection on problems of predication and participation which arose while he was a member of the Academy, especially, one imagines, the problem of the Dilemma of Partici-

---

[1] *Metaphysics*, I, 987b, 4 ff.

[2] This passage should be glossed by *Metaphysics*, VII, 1039b, 27 ff., where Aristotle issues a polemic against the possibility of defining sensibles, because they have matter whose nature is such that they are capable of being or not being. He then goes on to argue that Ideas, though eternal, are not definable either.

pation stated by Plato in the *Parmenides* (131a–c) and *Philebus* (15a–c). But Socrates could hardly have supposed that Forms were not individual. No doubt it would be difficult to turn up texts to prove this: a man does not in general testify to the lack of notions which have never crossed his mind. But the passages in the early dialogues which assume the existence of Forms also customarily assume their numerical oneness; to look no further than the *Protagoras*, justice is there a thing (πρᾶγμα τι, 330c; cf. 330d, 352d), virtue is a single thing (ἕν τι, 329c), and if the virtues are distinct from each other, each has its own peculiar nature and reality (τις ἴδιος οὐσία, 349b). Commitment to the existence of Forms in the early dialogues involves commitment to their individuality.

It remains to consider whether Aristotle, in denying that Socrates separated the Ideas, may not have meant that Socrates distinguished Forms from their instances, but that he did not regard them as independent of or prior to their instances. Once again there is no textual evidence that Aristotle meant this;[1] unlike his modern commentators, he does not suggest that the Socratic Form is 'immanent' in its instances.[2] But if Aristotle did mean this,

---

[1] See, however, *Metaphysics*, VII, 1042a, 26 ff., where Aristotle distinguishes two kinds of separation, one of which he himself accepts for certain forms. Individual material substances are separable in an unqualified sense, χωριστὸν ἁπλῶς; the forms of those substances, however, are separable in formula or definition, τῷ λόγῳ χωριστόν. Since, in attacking Plato on separation, Aristotle means to attack the notion that forms are χωριστὸν ἁπλῶς, it has been inferred that by denying that Socrates separated the Ideas, Aristotle meant to allow the possibility that Socrates viewed forms as separable in formula (and thus not identical with their instances), but did not view them as separate in an unqualified sense (and thus unable to exist independently of their instances).

But there is nothing to indicate that Aristotle meant any such thing; the name of Socrates is not mentioned in the passage. And though the sense of the expression 'separable in formula' is obscure (presumably, though not certainly, what is separable in formula may be defined without reference to perceptible matter, so that convex is separable in formula and snub is not, since the latter implies convexity of a nose; cf. 1023b 28 ff., 1035a 1 ff., 1037a 21 ff., 1064a 20 ff.) that from which the form is separable in formula is matter, and the form-matter distinction is Aristotle's, not Socrates'.

[2] At *Metaphysics* I 991a 8–18, Aristotle contrasts Plato's theory of Ideas with a theory of immanence which he attributes (not to Socrates but) to Anaxagoras and Eudoxus. As the passage itself suggests, and as Alexander of Aphrodisias' commentary on it, summarizing arguments of the περὶ Ἰδεῶν (and the *Parmenides*) shows (*in Meta*. 97.27–98.24 (Hayduck)) the sense of 'in' used is the sense in which part is in whole or an element of a mixture is in the mixture. The discussion is inapplicable to the early dialogues; see above, p. 75.

he was, so far as the early dialogues are concerned, mistaken; for the non-identity of Forms and their instances is there connected with the priority of Forms to their instances. Epistemologically, knowledge of Forms is prior to knowledge of what things have them, and also prior to knowledge of what properties happen to be connected with them. Ontologically, the priority of Forms is implied by the fact that they are essences and causes by which things are what they are; their existence is a condition for the existence of their instances. That priority implies existential independence. If Euthyphro's action in prosecuting his father is holy, its existence as holy depends upon the existence of the Form of holiness, by which it is holy; it would be merely queer to think that the Form of holiness depends for its existence on Euthyphro's action in prosecuting his father being holy.

To sum up: Aristotle, in denying that Socrates separated the Ideas, probably meant that Socrates did not distinguish Forms from their sensible instances. It is less likely that he meant that Socrates distinguished the Forms, but did not distinguish them as individuals, or that Socrates distinguished the Forms, but did not regard them as independent of and prior to their instances. But whichever of these things Aristotle meant, his testimony, applied to the early dialogues, is mistaken. By all of the criteria of separation which he suggests – non-identity, individuality, independence and priority – Forms are as 'separate' in the early dialogues as they are later on.

Aristotle's Authority

This conclusion will be questioned by those – and there are many – who have become accustomed to put great trust in Aristotle's authority as a commentator on Plato. Thus, for example, Mr. J. E. Raven, after suggesting that *Euthyphro*, 6d–e, sounds remarkably like a statement of the theory of Forms, dismisses this notion on the basis of 'the most important and authoritative of all our scraps of ancient evidence on this question':[1]

At *Metaphysics*, M, 1078b, 30, Aristotle writes in so many words: 'But whereas Socrates did not regard his universals as separable nor his definitions, they (i.e. Plato and his followers) attributed separate existence to them and gave to this class of realities the

[1] *Plato's Thought in the Making*, p. 39.

name of Ideas'. This passage, which follows almost immediately upon that to which I referred earlier to the effect that Socrates' two contributions to the history of philosophy were inductive reasoning and general definition, contains, just like the earlier sentence, a straightforward statement of fact. No use, therefore, to argue in this instance, as we fairly can in many other contexts, that Aristotle's criticism of his predecessors' views is invalidated by his avowed object of seeing what anticipations he can find in earlier thinkers of his own doctrines. Here we have, as I say, a bald statement of fact, not a prejudiced criticism. It is a fact, moreover, which Aristotle, if anybody, had every opportunity of knowing. For the best part of twenty years he was Plato's pupil in the Academy. It is inconceivable that during that time Plato's relations with Socrates should not have been often discussed or that Aristotle should have been wrong when he wrote these brief but vital sentences.

In applying this to the interpretation of *Euthyphro*, 6d–e, Mr. Raven assumes that Aristotle's account of the historical Socrates holds also for the Socrates of the early dialogues; and if those dialogues were a main source of Aristotle's information about Socrates, this is not unreasonable. Yet it hardly thereby follows that Aristotle's claims are true, and if they are mistaken, it is presumably conceivable that they are mistaken.

What should be made of the argument that Aristotle, having been Plato's pupil, could not have misunderstood him? It is an elderly argument, whose force has been effectively estimated by Professor Cherniss:[1]

> [C]ertainly there is no validity in the argument that, having been a student of Plato for twenty years, [Aristotle] *could* not have misunderstood him, for we have indications that on other questions the immediate pupils of Plato disagreed about the nature and import of his opinions . . . so that we are estopped from arguing that the interpretation of an immediate pupil must for that reason alone be correct.

Both Xenocrates and, as it would appear, Hermodorus,[2] gave accounts of Plato's views at variance with Aristotle's accounts. Nor need this be surprising. To the claim that the pupils of

---

[1] *ACPA*, p. 208; cf. pp. 87–8.
[2] *ap.* Simplicius, *Phys.*, 247, 30–248, 15; cf. Sextus, *Adv. Math.*, X, 261, and *PTI*, pp. 185–7.

philosophers may be relied upon to understand their teachers, one might oppose the claim, as a rule of thumb better founded on experience, that the more original and creative the pupil is as a philosopher in his own right, and the more dominating the initial influence of the teacher on him, the more likely misinterpretation in the long run will become: new vantage-points, especially when hard-gained, produce novel and sometimes distorted perspectives. Aristotle, it need hardly be said, was a most original and creative pupil; Plato, it need hardly be said, was a dominating influence on his thought.

Perhaps, then, it is only inconceivable that Aristotle is mistaken about Plato when he is making a 'straightforward statement of fact', as distinct from a prejudiced criticism. This distinction is not new, and neither is its refutation:[1]

> Must not [Aristotle's] reports, as distinguished from his interpretations, be considered unimpeachable testimony? Such is the plausible distinction adopted by A. E. Taylor... and John Burnet before him... who say that we are bound to believe Aristotle when he tells us that Plato *said* a particular thing, but not when he tells us what Plato *meant* or what the historical origin of a doctrine was. The plausibility of this neat distinction is considerably diminished, however, by common experience, which teaches that in spite of the best intentions a witness' testimony as to fact is deeply affected by his own unconscious interpretation of the fact. The applicability of the distinction is especially impaired in the case of Aristotle, who so interwined report, interpretation and criticism that even von Stein, who defended his account of Plato, asserted that his reports and his criticism are prejudiced by each other.... Moreover, other scholars have maintained that Aristotle not infrequently puts into the mouth of a philosopher what he considers the necessary implication of that philosopher's doctrine as he interprets it, and that he gives mistaken reports, not merely interpretations, of Platonic dialogues which are at our disposal.

What, after all, does it mean to say that Aristotle's claim that Socrates did not separate the Ideas is 'a bald statement of fact'? That it is a quotation from Plato or other companions of Socrates? There is no evidence of this. That it is *not* an interpretation, either of the early dialogues or the Academic tradition? There is

[1] *ACPA*, pp. xi–xii.

no evidence of this either, and to find such evidence would require a ground for distinguishing fact from interpretation which has yet to be sustained. It would seem, then, that the meaning to be assigned to the expression 'bald statement of fact', considerations of glabrescence apart, is merely that the statement is true. Since that is the point which Mr. Raven is attempting to establish, his argument is a *petitio*.

Aristotle, no doubt, was Plato's pupil. But then consider the quality of the testimony about Plato Aristotle provides. This may be illustrated, for specimen purposes, by his first survey of Plato's doctrines in the *Metaphysics* (I, ch. vi).[1]

Aristotle in this chapter provides four distinct kinds of evidence: (1) He testifies that Plato 'separated' changing sensible objects from the unchanging Forms in which they partake; and the dialogues, as well as the testimony of other immediate pupils of Plato,[2] provide ample evidence for his claim. (2) He testifies that Plato posited a class of 'intermediates', the objects of mathematics, between Forms and sensibles; and if this is not supported by the dialogues, there are at least scattered passages which have been so interpreted as to suggest it.[3] (3) He testifies to the existence of Idea Numbers, derived from 'the One' and 'the Great and the Small' or 'the Dyad', and this cannot be directly confirmed or disconfirmed by the dialogues.[4] (4) Finally, he testifies that Plato used only formal and material causes in explanation, and by implication denies that efficient and final causality have any role in his thought.[5] That is, Aristotle claims that the man who in the *Phaedrus* and *Laws* defined soul as self-moving motion, and held it to be the source of all other motion in the universe, had no place in his philosophy for an efficient cause. He claims that the

---

[1] For further discussion of this chapter, see *ACPA*, pp. 177–84; *REA*, pp. 6–8; Ross, *Aristotle's* Metaphysics, i, pp. 157–77.

[2] See *ACPA*, pp. 203–11 and nn. 121–5.

[3] Most recently by Anders Wedberg, *Plato's Philosophy of Mathematics*, pp. 92–135.

[4] Some scholars – for example, Henry Jackson (*Journal of Philology*, X (1882), pp. 277–84) – have claimed to find a derivation of the Ideas implied in the 'Mixed Class' of the *Philebus* (23c–27c); this is mistaken, as Ross (*PTI*, pp. 133–5) points out. It is notorious that this passage of the *Philebus*, along with the deductions of the *Parmenides*, is difficult to connect with the theory of Ideas, and apparently raised questions among Plato's immediate pupils. Much of what Aristotle has to say about the One and the indefinite Dyad appears to rest on a misinterpretation of *Parmenides*, 143a–145a.   [5] 992a, 29 ff.; cf. *PTI*, pp. 233–9.

man who in the *Phaedo* said that sensible objects strive to be like Forms, and in the *Republic* defined the Good as the first principle of existence and intelligibility, and in the *Timaeus* proclaimed the world a work of rational design, had no place in his philosophy for a final cause. This testimony suffers from a cardinal defect: it is incredible.

There are ways to make the incredible palatable. For example, one may jettison the text of Plato. Perhaps the 'exoteric' Plato published dialogues, more or less misleading as to his true views, for a popular audience (which must have relished the *Parmenides*), while the 'esoteric' Plato reserved his more intimate and advanced theories, the 'unwritten doctrines',[1] for his students in the Academy. We may then suppose, relying on Aristotle, that the exoteric Plato proclaimed a Divine Maker in the *Timaeus* because the esoteric Plato thought it good for the troops.[2]

This approach has at least one sterling advantage: consistently applied, no appeal to the text of Plato can refute it. Those who find virtue in this fact are unlikely to be dissuaded by the further fact that, whereas Plato's dialogues contain a body of thought which has moved the world, the reconstruction of his beliefs from Aristotle's testimony, even when undertaken by philosophically competent hands, has generally some appearance of gibberish. It is surely preferable, however, to assume that Aristotle's testimony is sometimes radically inaccurate, and inaccurate on the most fundamental aspects of Plato's thought. When his testimony cannot be measured against an independent control, it is insufficient warrant for Plato's views.[3]

[1] Mentioned by Aristotle at *Physics*, IV, 209b, 13–16.

[2] Mr. Konrad Gaiser (*Platons Ungeschriebene Lehre*, p. 3) has recently reaffirmed a contrast between *einer innerschulischen Forschung und Lehre* (*Esoterik*) and *einer für die politische Öffentlichkeit bestimmten Schriftstellerei* (*Exoterik*). The dialogues, he claims, do not represent Plato's own philosophy, or genuine philosophical *Erkenntnis*; they portray an idealized Socrates presenting protreptical speeches in the form of literary art-works. The task of the interpreter is to penetrate beyond Plato's text to the *esoterischen Zentrums der platonischen Philosophie*, to get at its *tieferen Sinn*. See also H. J. Kramer, *Arete bei Platon und Aristotles*, ch. iv.

[3] The distinction between the evidential worth of Aristotle's reports and his interpretations was coined precisely to get around this. But it fails to provide a criterion for distinguishing. There are a few circumstances in which Aristotle says he is *quoting* Plato; but these are rare. In most cases, there is no textual basis for applying the distinction, and this is specifically true of the whole of *Metaphysics*, I, vi. If that chapter is construed as an interpretation rather than a report, almost everything which

It will follow from this that if Plato proclaimed 'unwritten doctrines' in the Academy, we cannot now determine on the basis of Aristotle's testimony what those doctrines were. This is not, of course, to say that 'all that Aristotle says about Plato that cannot be verified from the dialogues is pure misunderstanding or misrepresentation'.[1] It is rather to say that all that Aristotle says about Plato that cannot be verified from the dialogues cannot be known *not* to be pure misunderstanding or misrepresentation. The issue is evidential.[2]

This is not to say that Aristotle wilfully or consciously misrepresented Plato; that view is absurd. But Aristotle as a philosopher, like Hegel, used the work of previous philosophers dialectically, as stepping-stones for the development of his own views;[3] and, again like Hegel, he tended to regard the work of his predecessors as mere anticipations of the truth he had now won through to proclaim. All of this is no doubt right and proper. Philosophers have always used the history of their subject as a

---

[1] As Ross (*PTI*, p. 143) represents Cherniss's view.

[2] Professor Guthrie, defending Aristotle's historical sense in discussing the Presocratics, remarks: '. . . it is far from my intention to argue that Aristotle was a faultless historian or that we can never be in a position to see his faults. He can certainly be detected in misinterpretation, and sometimes in self-contradiction, on the subject of an earlier philosopher. But to put it at its lowest, he was intellectually mature, and the fault must in each case be proved before it can be assumed' (*Journal of Hellenic Studies*, lxxvii, (1) (1957), pp. 38–9). This is an argument from burden of proof, and, at least when applied to Aristotle on Plato, an unconvincing one. Measured by the evidence of the dialogues, some of Aristotle's testimony is true, and some is false; in cases where the dialogues are silent, we have no ground for deciding what testimony is true and what false. Where there is no ground for decision, there is no burden of proof. If we ask, for example, how many Persians killed at Marathon were bald, the burden of proof rests neither on him who holds there were fifty, nor on him who holds there were none. In such matters as these, the issue is not burden of proof, but onus of answering.

[3] F. M. Cornford remarked (*PTK*, p. 31): '. . . A modern reader is likely to be misled. He will expect a philosopher who criticizes another philosopher to feel himself bound by the historical question, what that other philosopher actually meant. But neither Plato nor Aristotle is writing the history of philosophy; rather, they are philosophizing and concerned only to obtain what light they can from any quarter. We can never assume, as a matter of course, that the construction they put upon the doctrines of other philosophers is faithful to historical fact.'

Aristotle has to say about Plato, in the *Metaphysics* and elsewhere, will follow it to the dustbin. If that chapter is construed as a report rather than an interpretation, the conflict between Aristotle's testimony and Plato's text is unresolved.

vehicle for its advancement, made their predecessors party to their argument. When this tactic produces philosophy worth having – as it surely did in Aristotle's case – it is worth pursuing. But to proceed in this way almost inevitably leads to interpretations which are historically unsound, and sometimes monstrous, for it requires that earlier schemes of thought be viewed against the background of alien questions and assumptions. This is why Aristotle's testimony so often has the quality that it has;[1] and one might almost suppose that he would not have been an original philosopher had it been otherwise.

There are a variety of reasons why Aristotle's testimony has so often been accorded undue weight in the interpretation of Plato. One is the strength, in many quarters, of an antique tradition. Those who accept the Neoplatonic interpretation of Plato may well value Aristotle's testimony as evidence for their views, since Plato, read through Aristotle's eyes, has much in him of Plotinus. The Neoplatonic interpretation has not, in general, gained wide support among English-speaking scholars, who distrust its implied mysticism. Still, it has a claim to being the oldest part of the scholarly tradition. During the Middle Ages and the Renaissance, it was what 'Platonism' meant, and, partly no doubt due to the influence of Hegel and German Romanticism, it remains a major motif in much Continental scholarship. Its treatment of Aristotle's testimony has established itself over generations, and developed, apparently, an independent life of its own.

A second reason is a doctrine of privileged access: it is assumed that Plato lectured in the Academy, that Aristotle heard him, and that Aristotle's testimony to what he heard, with all its faults, is all we have. The evidence on which this rests is a single passage of Aristoxenus, describing the audience which came to hear a lecture by Plato on the Good:[2]

---

[1] Cherniss has suggested that the whole of Aristotle's testimony as to Idea Numbers has this origin (*REA*, pp. 29–30): 'Let those who think it overbold to suggest that the theory of idea numbers was not a theory of Plato's at all, but an interpretation of Aristotle's, consider Aristotle's assertion that Leucippus and Democritus, too, make all entities numbers and derived from numbers. That they do not state this clearly he admits; but he insists that this is what they really mean, for Aristotle is one of those who cannot be refuted by an author's words because he is sure that the author was unable to say what he really thought.'

[2] *Harm. El.*, ii, 30–1, cited and translated by Ross, *PTI*, pp. 147–8. Brackets added.

They came, every one of them, in the conviction that they would get from the lecture[s] some one or other of the things that the world calls good; riches or health, or strength – in fine, some extraordinary gift of fortune. But when they found that Plato's reasonings were of mathematics – numbers, geometry, and astronomy – and, to crown all, to the effect that there is one Good, methinks their disenchantment was complete. The result was that some of them sneered at the thing, while others vilified it.

The lecture[s] referred to were public: members of the Academy would have been prepared for what they got. And, given the popular reaction, it would be surprising indeed if Plato gave many of them.[1] But there is a certain irony, which has its own delight, in the picture of Plato lecturing on mathematics and metaphysics to an audience who came to improve their health, strengthen their muscles, and get rich quick.

It has often been claimed that Aristotle got his knowledge of the theory of Idea Numbers from this Lecture. But Plato surely would not have revealed his deepest thoughts on metaphysics to a popular audience, untrained in mathematics and dialectic, if he did not reveal those thoughts in the later dialogues – dialogues far too technical and difficult for general publication, and written with members of his own Academy in view. The 'unwritten doctrines' traced to this lecture are not of the sort that any sensible man would broadcast to an ignorant multitude – if,

[1] Ross (*PTI*, p. 148) is convinced that we have here a report of a series of lectures, and indeed a course of lectures. The reception described by Aristoxenus makes this difficult to believe; see also, *? Epistle VII*, 341e-342a, which, whether or not Plato's own words, confirms Aristoxenus. Ross argues from the fact that Simplicius, Philoponus, and Aesclepius, three commentators on Aristotle writing some eight hundred years after the event, sometimes use the plurals λόγοι, and συνουσίαι in referring to it. This, if it is not contradicted, is surely not supported by the text of Aristoxenus, for ἀκρόασιν, the word Ross translates 'lectures', is singular. Ross holds that the singular may mean a course of lectures, as in Φυσικὴ ἀκρόασις, but gives no examples to show that this is true in the absence of the modifying adjective. Cf. *REA*, p. 2: 'Yet in most of the authoritative treatments of Plato, after a scholarly reference to this lecture on the Good, the singular becomes an unexplained plural within the paragraph, the lecture a whole series of lectures, and before the section has been finished we are being told that Plato gave "regular lectures", "systematic and continuous expositions in lecture form on some of the most important points in his doctrine". This "expansion" of the evidence – if I may use the term – has been embellished by the different expositors with different details, a comparison of which would afford a certain cynical amusement to the historian of critical scholarship.'

indeed, they are of the sort that a sensible man would broadcast at all. But to say this is to say that there is no evidence whatever that Plato expounded ultimate metaphysical views by means of lectures, because Aristoxenus provides the only direct evidence for a lecture that we have.[1]

But there is another and more pervasive element at work in the use of Aristotle as a primary witness for Plato's thought. This is the apparently ineradicable psychologism which infects the study of the history of philosophy. The student of Plato, it is supposed, has as his object the discovery of Plato's thoughts – that is, his entertained beliefs. What Plato wrote is merely evidence for those beliefs. But there is another source of evidence which is independent of what Plato wrote – namely Aristotle's testimony. Since what Plato wrote sometimes conflicts with what Aristotle says he believed, it is the task of the historian somehow to adjudicate the dispute, weighing these two classes of partially inconsistent evidence in order to strike a balance: the balance representing historical fact – namely, what Plato *really* believed. We are then well on our way to belief in esoteric doctrines, the reconstruction of which may provide much pleasure and amusement.

But it is possible, after all, to choose another way of proceeding. It is possible to treat Plato's text, not as evidence for something else, but as itself the primary object of historical understanding. The aim of inquiry is then to interpret a set of literary documents, not to fathom the entertained beliefs of their author. It is reasonable, of course, to assume that the documents are a reliable index to the beliefs; but the connection, after all, is contingent, and as far as interpretation is concerned, unimportant.[2] If Plato, in his

---

[1] This, of course, is not to deny that Plato taught. At *Phaedrus*, 275c–277b (see also *? Epistle VII*, 341b–d), the written word is said to serve only as a reminder of the truth, an image of the living *logos* put forward by the man who knows through dialectic. The operative word here, surely, is *dialectic*: there is nothing to indicate that Plato's teaching was different in kind, or markedly different in content, from that teaching of which the dialogues are a *mimesis*. If so, then Aristotle faced the same kind of interpretative problems we also face.

[2] You pick up the Oxford text of Plato – token of a lot of type – and use the set of sentences it contains as evidence for a theory. Is your theory about what went on in the head of the antique Athenian who wrote the sentences? Or is it about what those sentences mean, what statements or propositions they express? The general view, I suppose, is that the theories (interpretations) of historians of philosophy are intentional statements of the form, 'S believed *p*', where S is a dead philosopher

heart of hearts, had been a nominalist, an atheist, a sceptic about immortality, and a hedonist, and had yet gone on to write the dialogues which he wrote for some obscure motive now unknown, this would not change the proper interpretation of what he wrote and privately disbelieved by one iota: when a man says what he does not believe, we may still perfectly well understand what it is he has said. The question, then, of whether Plato had beliefs he did not express, or beliefs contrary to what he did express, may be left to those with skill in the arts of divination; the historian may more reasonably limit himself to the study of texts and their meaning. If inquiry is construed in this way, it is self-referentially inconsistent to prefer the testimony of Aristotle to the evidence of Plato's text in the interpretation of Plato.

The Immanence of Forms

The fact that Forms in the early dialogues are not identical with their instances and prior to their instances militates against the claim that they are 'in' their instances. Professor Ross has maintained that, in the development of the theory of Forms, 'there is a general movement away from immanence to transcendence. In the early period almost everything speaks of immanence.'[1] In later dialogues, he holds, particulars are conceived as never fully exemplifying or instantiating their Forms; they only imitate them. But in the early dialogues, the Form is treated 'as being immanent in particular things. It is "present" in them; it is placed "in them" by the craftsman; it comes to be "in them"; it is "common" to them; the particulars, in turn, "possess" it or "share in" it.'[2]

The force of this claim turns on the meaning of 'immanent'.

[1] *PTI*, p. 230.
[2] *PTI*, p. 21.

---

and *p* is something he believed. This is the view I have called psychologism, on the analogy of psychologism in logic, which identifies the mental act of inference with the relation of implication. To it may be opposed the claim that the theories of historians of philosophy – unless they are writing biography – are of the form, 'S means *p*', where S is a sentence or set of sentences, and *p* is what those sentences mean. Perhaps there is no need to invent a lofty honorific to describe studying the history of philosophy without psychologism, if it is merely studying the history of philosophy.

All of the expressions Professor Ross cites are used quite ordinarily in Greek with abstract nouns;[1] to say, for example, that there is justice in an action is merely another way, and an ordinary way, of saying that an action is just. Since Forms are the meanings of abstract nouns, the use of such expressions is metaphysically neutral: if the claim that Forms are immanent in their instances merely summarizes facts of linguistic usage, the claim is true but, so far as the issue of ontological status is concerned, vacuous.

On the other hand, if 'immanent' is taken to ascribe an ontological status to Forms, rather than as a mere blanket-word covering certain uses of language, Professor Ross's appeal to the language of the early dialogues will not support his claim that Forms are there immanent. Nor is it possible to define this nonordinary sense of immanence in terms of its putative opposite, transcendence: the claim that Forms are in some technical sense 'in' things cannot be fixed by the denial that they are 'separate' or 'apart', because Professor Ross treats immanence and transcendence, not as contraries, but as complementaries. The reason for this is that Plato uses the 'in' locution and its congeners in the middle and later dialogues, just as he had earlier on, and Professor Ross infers from this that:[2]

---

[1] See above, pp. 115–16. This is true even of the expressions for sharing, which may at first sight seem technical. For further discussion, see H. C. Baldry, *Classical Quarterly*, xxxi (1937), pp. 145–6. The use of the metaphors of presence with abstract nouns is as old as Homer: Cf. αἰδὼς ... παρεῖναι, *Od.* xvii, 347, quoted at *Charmides*, 161a.

[2] *PTI*, p. 231. Ross bases his conclusion on the tables offered on pp. 228–30. As Cherniss has pointed out (*SPM*, p. 363), those tables are incomplete; they neither cite all occurrences of terms considered, nor consider all relevant terms. In particular, they do not cite the occurrence of terms and constructions which presumably indicate 'transcendence' in the early dialogues — namely, those which suggest that the connection between Forms and their instances is somehow causal. See above, pp. 122–23.

Professor Ross had earlier maintained that Forms must both be immanent and transcendent in *Aristotle's Metaphysics*, vol. i, p. xli, where he ascribed this interpretation to Aristotle. Forms are immanent because 'the Platonic doctrine of the participation of the particulars in the Ideas ... implies the presence of the Idea as an element in particulars'. They are transcendent because Plato's use of the metaphors of imitation in describing the relation between Forms and particulars expresses 'belief in the existence of universals quite apart from individual instances' (p. xlii). But this contrast between participation and imitation is not Aristotle's, for Aristotle claims that, 'the Pythagoreans say that things exist by "imitation" of

The only conclusion possible seems to be that, while he [Plato] was not quite satisfied with either expression, he saw no way of getting nearer to the truth than by using both, the one stressing the intimacy of the link between a universal and its particulars, the other stressing the failure of every particular to be a perfect exemplification of any universal. He may even have had an inkling that the relation is completely unique and indefinable. Both 'sharing' and 'imitating' are metaphors for it, and the use of two complementary metaphors is better than the sole use of either.

The conclusion is hard to follow. If exemplification is a relation *sui generis*, capable of no analysis and in need of none, then 'imitating' and 'sharing' can hardly be useful metaphors for it; metaphor implies some sort of analogous relationship, and there is here no ground for an analogy. It may be added that since 'sharing' is, as 'imitating' is not, used quite ordinarily with abstract nouns, it is not in the strict sense a metaphor at all. But beyond that immanence cannot be defined as the denial of transcendence, and Professor Ross nowhere succeeds in giving the term an independent meaning of its own. It is both true and important that in the middle and later dialogues, Forms are only deficiently exemplified by the instances which imitate them; and there is no reason why that state of affairs should not be called 'transcendence' if one chooses. But because no independent meaning has been assigned to 'immanence', neither truth not falsity attach to Professor Ross's claim that Forms are immanent in their instances in the early dialogues, if that claim is meant as an account of their ontological status.

The truth of the matter is that in a strong sense of term Forms are as 'separate' from their instances in the early dialogues as they are later on. For they are not identical with their instances, and ontologically prior to their instances. That is, they exist 'apart'. The difference between the theory of Forms in the early dialogues and those which followed does not consist in the fact of separation, but the way in which separation is conceived. The middle dialogues present a revised estimate of ontological status, an estimate which turns on a theory of the way in which Forms are.

---

numbers, and Plato says they exist by participation, changing the name. But what the participation or the imitation of the Forms could be they left an open question' (*Meta.*, I, 987b, 10 ff.). Professor Ross bases his distinction on what Aristotle explicitly refuses to distinguish. Cf. J. D. Mabbott, *Classical Quarterly*, xx (1926), p. 73.

Separation in the Phaedo

The theme of separation is first introduced in the *Phaedo* through a contrast between sensation and reflection. Socrates begins by eliciting Simmias' agreement that there exists such a thing as justice, alone by itself, and also beauty and goodness. He then argues that such things cannot be grasped by sight or any other sense, but only by pure thought, alone by itself. Sensation is inferior to reflection in the search for knowledge (*Phaedo*, 65d–e).

By a natural extension, this account provokes a corollary: that the objects of sensation are inferior to the objects of reflection. This is the core of the second argument for Recollection in the *Phaedo*, whose initial premise is that there exists a Form of equality (74a–b):

> We say, I suppose, that there is something equal – I do not mean as stick is equal to stick or stone to stone or anything of that sort, but something else over and beyond all these things – the equal itself.

It is then shown that equality and sensible equals are ἕτερα ὄντα, different sorts of things; for sensible equals prove equal to one thing, but not to another,[1] whereas things which are just equal cannot be unequal, nor equality inequality (74b–c). Equality and equal things, then, differ in that equality cannot be qualified by inequality, whereas sensible equals may also be unequal.

Having shown that equality is not to be identified with its sensible instances, the *Phaedo* next goes on to characterize their relationship. It is agreed that sensible equals are not equal as equality is equal, but fall short of being of such sort as it is; they wish to be of such sort as another sort of thing, but are inferior to it; they resemble it, but are deficient with respect to it (74d–e). But, since we are able to recognize this deficiency, it must follow that we had previous knowledge of equality in and of itself (75b):

> Before we began to see or hear or use any of the other senses, we must have had knowledge of what the equal itself is, if we are able to refer these sensible equals to that object, on the ground that all such things are striving to be of such sort as that, but are inferior to it.

---

[1] Reading τῷ ... τῷ in 74b, 8–9, since τότε ... τότε is excluded by ἐνίοτε, and construing the datives as parallel to those in 74a, 10. The argument may be glossed by *Republic*, VII, 523a–524c; cf. V, 479a–c.

We cannot, so to speak, *abstract* our knowledge of equality from sensible equals, because of their deficiency; rather, we must have that knowledge in order to recognize that sensible equals are equals. The same account holds true of (75c–d):

> The greater and the less and everything of that sort, for our argument applies no less to equality than to beauty itself, to the good itself, to justice, holiness, and in a word, to all those things which, in our dialectic, we ratify with the seal of reality.

The inferiority of sensation to reflection is to be explained in terms of the inferiority of sensible instances to intelligible Forms.

Separation here plainly involves something more than the non-identity, independence, or priority. It involves the claim that instances of Forms are deficient imitations or resemblances of Forms. To borrow a phrase from Professor Vlastos, it involves a Copy-Theory.[1] To that theory was later conjoined, as a natural corollary, the theory that sensibles and Forms differ in their degree of reality, that Forms are more real than their instances.[2]

The Two Worlds

The *Phaedo* goes on to develop the distinction between sensible and intelligible objects into a doctrine of Two Worlds, Visible and Invisible. Like knows like, and the rational soul is akin to the objects of its knowledge, which are eternal. The objects of the Visible World, 'those things which are named after what is real', are in a perpetually changing mortal realm, never the same with respect to each other or themselves. By contrast, Forms, the reality of whose existence we render an account in questioning and answering, exist always in the same way with respect to the same things, single in nature, alone by themselves, never in any way under any circumstances admitting alteration (78d–79b).

In the *Republic*, the Two Worlds become the Worlds of Knowledge and Opinion. Socrates there undertakes to define the philosopher, the lover of wisdom, and to distinguish him from the lovers of beautiful sights and sounds who superficially resemble him. The discussion begins by assuming the theory of Forms (V, 475e–476a):

[1] 'The Third Man Argument in the Parmenides', *SPM*, p. 242.
[2] *Republic*, V, 475e ff.; cf. Vlastos, *op. cit.*, 247–8.

> I believe you will agree with me that, since beautiful is opposite
> to ugly, they are two things; and therefore, each of them is one.
> The same is true of justice and injustice, good and evil, and all of
> the characters. Each is one thing by itself, but through intercourse
> with actions and bodies and each other, each appears many by
> appearing in many places.

It is recognition of the Form of beauty which distinguishes
philosophers from the lovers of sights and sounds; the latter are
living in a dream. Dreaming, whether awake or asleep, is believing
that what is like something is not merely like it, but the very
thing it resembles. The philosopher, because he is able to discern
the distinction between beauty and the things which partake of it,
is awake and not dreaming, has knowledge and not mere opinion
(476c–d).

This likeness implies degrees of reality. What is fully knowable
is fully real (476e–477a). If, then, there is something such that
it both is and is not, it will lie between the fully real and the
wholly unreal. Since knowledge corresponds to the real, and
ignorance to the unreal, we must expect that if there is something
intermediate between reality and unreality, there is something
intermediate between knowledge and ignorance. This is opinion
or belief; for opinion is clearer than ignorance and more obscure
than knowledge (477a–b). Knowledge and opinion are different
powers or faculties, distinguished both by the state of mind they
produce and by their objects (477c–d). The state of mind produced by knowledge is infallible, and that produced by opinion
is fallible. The object of knowledge is the real, and its power that
of knowing the real as it is; the object of opinion cannot be unreal,
since that is nothing, and so must be something intermediate
between the real and the unreal (478a–d).

What is that object? To answer this question, we must turn to
those who recognize the existence of beautiful things, but deny
the existence of a Form of beauty, existing always the same in
respect to the same things, and ask (479a–b):

> Which of the many beautiful things will not also prove to be
> ugly? Or just things which are not unjust? Or holy things which
> are not unholy? The many doubles prove to be halves as well as
> doubles. Things large are small; things light are heavy, no more
> one thing than the opposite. Whatever each of these many things
> are said to be, they may just as well be said not to be. . . . They

are ambiguous, and it is impossible to form a steadfast conception of them either as being or as not being, as both, or as neither.

The objects of opinion are sensibles, which are not fully real nor yet nothing.

This account of Two Worlds rests on a series of proportions: as dreaming stands to waking, so opinion stands to knowledge, the more obscure stands to the clear, the less real stands to the real, and instances of Forms stand to Forms. In *Republic*, X, 597a, the carpenter is said not to make the Form of bed, but to make something which only resembles that Form; it is mistaken to call his production a perfectly real thing, because it is dim, indistinct, and feeble with respect to reality and truth.

The Two Worlds recur in a later dialogue, the *Timaeus*:[1]

> What is that which is always real and has no becoming, and what is that which is always becoming and is never real? That which is apprehensible by thought with a rational account is the thing that is always unchangeably real; whereas that which is the object of belief together with unreasoning sensation is the thing that becomes and passes away, but never has real being.

Being stands to Becoming as the intelligible stands to the sensible.

This is high metaphysics; but it is also, and importantly, a moral and religious doctrine, stressing the kinship between what is highest in the universe and what is deepest in the human soul. In the *Symposium*, the lover, in his search for beauty, ascends to another world; and in describing the nature or essence of Beauty found there, Plato's prose suddenly bursts into dithyrambs, in the manner of a choric ode (211a–b):

> First, it always is and does not come to be or perish;
> Nor has it growth or diminution.
> Again, it is not in one respect beautiful but in another not;
> Nor at one time beautiful but another not;
> Nor beautiful in one relation but ugly in another;
> Nor beautiful here but ugly there,
> As being beautiful to one man but not to another.

Nor again will it appear beautiful
In the manner of face or hands or parts of the body;
Nor beautiful as knowledge is beautiful, and argument;

[1] 27d–28a, trans. Cornford.

Nor beautiful as what is somewhere in something is beautiful,
As in an animal, or in Earth, or in Heaven, or in anything else:

> But it is what it is alone by itself,
> Single in nature forever.
> All other beautiful things share in it,
> In such manner that they come to be and perish.
> But it comes to be neither in greater degree nor less,
> And it is not affected.

This is a metaphysical description which is also a hymn. Plato's style quickens under the impulse of certain ideas; it is impossible to preserve in translation the pounding beat of his rhythms, the beat of the dance.

The soul of the lover who has attained to this height of vision is transformed (*Symposium*, 212a):

> There only it will befall him, in seeing Beauty by that through which it can alone be seen, to give birth. He will give birth, not to an image of virtue, since he does not touch an image, but to true virtue, since he touches the truth. And in giving birth to true virtue, and nurturing it, he becomes dear to god; and he, if any man, is immortal.

The metaphor of birth connects naturally with the metaphors of intercourse and marriage used in the *Republic*:[1]

> The true lover of knowledge [is] one born to strive towards reality, who cannot linger among that multiplicity of things which men believe to be real, but holds on his way with a passion that will not faint or fail until he has laid hold upon the essential nature of each thing with that part of his soul which can apprehend reality because of its affinity therewith; and when he has by that means approached real being and entered into union with it, the offspring of this marriage is intelligence and truth; so that at last, having found knowledge and true life and nourishment, he is at rest from his travail.

Plato's emphasis in the *Symposium* and *Republic* on vision and rebirth has a certain analogy to the ritual of the Eleusinian Mysteries, which celebrated fertility and purification, and culminated in a Beholding, or *Epopteia*, where the sacred objects

---

[1] *Republic*, VI, 490a–b, trans. Cornford.

of the cult were exposed to the wondering eyes of the worshippers suddenly, in a blaze of light, and the worshippers were assured of their kinship to the god and their salvation.

The doctrine of Two Worlds also has an analogy to the religious vision of Aeschylus:[1]

> In the stage observable in Aeschylus' latest plays, the choral part is still dramatic, and of equal importance with the dialogue. The two elements are evenly balanced; but at the same time they have begun to occupy different worlds, so that we are sensible of the transition from one to the other. The result is a curious duplication of the drama which now has two aspects, the one universal and timeless, the other particular and temporal.
>
> The nature of this phenomenon will, we hope, become clear, if we take as an illustration the *Agamemnon*. In this play, the visible presentation shows how the conquerer of Troy came home and was murdered by the queen. The events that go forward on the stage are *particular* events, located at a point of legendary time and of real space. The characters are certain individuals, legendary or historic – there is to Aeschylus no difference here – who lived at that moment and trod that spot of earth. But in the choral odes the action is lifted out of time and place on to the plane of the universal. When the stage is clear and the visible presentation is for the time suspended, then, above and beyond the transient spectacle of a few suffering mortals caught, just there and then, in the net of crime, loom up in majestic distance and awful outline the truths established, more unchangeably than the mountains, in the eternal counsels of Zeus. The pulse of momentary passion dies down; the clash and conflict of human wills, which just now had held us in breathless concentration, sink and dwindle to the scale of a puppet-show; while the enduring song of Destiny unrolls the theme of blood-haunted Insolence lured by insistent Temptation into the toils of Doom. As though on a higher stage, uncurtained in the choral part, another company of actors concurrently plays out a more majestic and symbolic drama. On this invisible scene walk the figures of Hybris and Peitho, of Nemesis and Ate – not the bloodless abstractions of later allegory, but still clothed in the glowing lineaments of supernatural reality. The curtain lifts for a timeless moment on the spectacle of human life in an aspect known to the all-seeing eyes of Zeus; and when it drops again, we turn back to the mortal tragedy of Agamemnon and Clytemnestra, enlightened, purified, uplifted, calm.

[1] F. M. Cornford, *Thucydides Mythistoricus*, pp. 144–5.

Both Plato and Aeschylus proclaimed the existence of a moral order, governing the workings of the common world; both treat that order as in some sense 'separate', having a reality of its own. For Plato, the elements of that order were found mainly in geometry and the moral virtues; the forces which walk the higher stage are Equality and Wisdom, Goodness and Beauty, not Hybris and Nemesis. The thought of Aeschylus moves within the scheme of an allied, but older, pattern of ideas, a scheme which had its roots in myths more ancient than philosophy and perhaps more ancient than Greece.

The Unity of Plato's Thought

Forms in the early dialogues are separated from their instances, in that they are not identical with them and ontologically prior to them. This remains true later on. But the middle dialogues expand this separation into a new view of the universe, involving a doctrine of Two Worlds, separated by a gulf of deficiency and unreality. Associated with this doctrine is a religious attitude unlike anything the early dialogues can show; for nowhere in the early dialogues is it suggested or implied that a Form – any Form – may be an appropriate object of worship. There is then a change – or more accurately, a development – in the theory of Forms between the early and the middle dialogues.

This claim will be rejected by those who maintain, as some of the most distinguished Platonists of this century have maintained, that Plato's thought is a unity, and that the theory of Forms found in the *Euthyphro* and other early dialogues is essentially the same as that of the *Phaedo* and *Republic*. Three main texts, drawn from the *Euthyphro*, the *Laches*, and the *Lysis*, have been used to support this view.

The *Euthyphro* assumes that Forms may be used as standards, and that the definition of a Form as a standard cannot imply that it is qualified by its own opposite. These are essential elements in the Copy-Theory of the *Phaedo*; but they do not establish the unitarian thesis. It is one thing to say that a Form may be used as a standard, and another to say that it may be so used because it is an exemplar of which its instances are deficient examples.[1] There is no hint in the *Euthyphro* that every instance of holiness must

[1] See *PTI*, p. 230.

somehow be deficiently holy; and it is clearly one thing to argue that a Form cannot be qualified by its own opposite, and another to argue that every instance of a Form may be qualified both by it and its opposite. It is the latter claim that is made in the middle dialogues, and which is essential for deficiency of resemblance.

The *Laches* contains an account of knowledge which makes it timeless, in the sense that it applies indifferently to past, present, and future (198d–199e). It has been held that the timelessness of knowledge implies the eternity of its objects, and that eternity implies complete reality, as opposed to the diminished reality of things which come to be and pass away. This inference, if sound, would support the unitarian thesis. But clearly, it is one thing to hold that knowledge is timeless as applying to past, present, and future, and another to hold that it must therefore have objects which are eternal; there is no evidence to show that Plato connected these claims in the early dialogues.

Again, there is the *Lysis*, where all valuable things are said to be images of the Primary Valuable, and described in such a way as to suggest deficiency. As the *Phaedo* maintains that 'Each of the Forms exist, and the other things, because they come to have a share of them, are named after them',[1] so the *Lysis* maintains that 'In speaking of things which are valuable for the sake of something else which is valuable, we seem to be uttering a mere phrase; the really valuable is that thing itself in which all these so-called valuable things terminate' (*Lysis* 220a–b). What appears to be at issue here is the primary and derivative designation of names, or eponymy, and this is an important linguistic corollary of the doctrine of Two Worlds. But the relation of valuable things to the primary valuable in the *Lysis* is not the relation of instances of Forms to Forms, for the former relation is, as the latter is not, the relation of means to ends; holy things are holy *by* holiness, but they are not holy *for the sake of* holiness, as, in the *Lysis*, medicine is valuable for the sake of health. Socrates in the *Lysis* is concerned with ethics and the goals of choice,[2] not with metaphysics. The *Lysis*, then, assumes a theory of naming which was later in the *Phaedo* applied to Forms; but it does not assume the *Phaedo's* theory of Forms, and the deficiency it attributes to means in relation to ends is not the deficiency of particulars. The

---

[1] *Phaedo*, 102b.

[2] Compare *E.N.*, I, 1094a, 18 ff.

Gorgias (467d) puts the *Lysis'* point in another way: 'If a man does something for a purpose, he does not wish the thing he does, but that for which he does it.'

The three passages generally cited in support of the unitarian account of the theory of Forms do not imply that that account is true. But there is another argument to be considered. That is that even if Plato did not state the middle theory of Forms in the early dialogues, it is an argument from silence to infer that he therefore did not hold it. A man need not tell everything he knows every time he writes.

This argument would have more force if it could be shown that the theory of Forms in the early dialogues implies the deficiency and diminished reality of instances of Forms; Plato was presumably at least as capable of tracing such implications as we are. But no such implication exists. On the contrary: deficiency and diminished reality are connected in the middle dialogues with problems of knowledge not discussed in the early dialogues, and with solutions to those problems which are inconsistent with claims maintained earlier on.

Thus, for example, the claim of diminished reality is used in the *Republic* as a means of distinguishing the objects of knowledge from those of opinion. But the very distinction between knowledge and opinion is not put earlier than the *Meno* (97a–98b);[1] and the claim that knowledge and opinion have different objects is not only absent from the *Meno*, but implicitly contradicted by it, since opinion is there turned into knowledge by 'reflection on the reason' (98a; cf. 85c).

Again, the *Phaedo* holds that the claims that Forms exist and that our souls existed before birth are equivalent (76d–e), and the basis of this is the doctrine of Recollection, which in turn rests on the deficiency of instances of Forms to Forms. But in the early dialogues, Socrates, so far from accepting the claims of immortality made in the *Phaedo* – claims which can scarcely be ignored if the doctrine of Recollection and the doctrine of deficiency are true – is agnostic. For in the *Apology* (20c–21d), speaking to the friends and sympathizers who had voted for his acquittal, and with no motive for distorting his personal views, Socrates is willing to claim of death only that there is reason to think it a good, since

---

[1] If one excepts the *Gorgias*, 454c ff., which Professor Dodds (*Gorgias*, p. 23) dates somewhat earlier than the *Meno*.

it is *either* a state of nothingness and unconsciousness, like a profound and dreamless sleep, *or* a passage of the soul from this world to another, conceived after the fashion of Homer. These are not the words of a man glowing with the hot conviction of the *Phaedo* that the soul is immortal, and will exist after death 'alone by itself'.

There is, of course, a unity to Plato's thought; but it is not the unity of a monument. It is the unity of growth and development, the unity of life.

Motives for Change

If it is true that the early and the middle dialogues differ in their assessment of the status of Forms, it is worth asking how that difference is to be explained. What philosophical motives prompted it? In both the early and the middle dialogues, Forms are 'separate'. But 'separation', as between those groups of dialogues, has different senses. Forms are separate in the early dialogues as being distinct from and prior to their instances. They are separate in the middle dialogues as being fully real exemplars of which their instances are deficient and less real examples. It should follow that the questions of ontological status Plato meant to answer in the middle dialogues differ from those asked earlier on, and this in fact is true. Plato's account in the middle dialogues is conditioned by problems in epistemology which the early dialogues had not faced. Those problems arose over scepticism and *a priori* knowledge. They arose, not *in* Socratic dialectic, but *about* it; specifically, they arose when Plato turned to deal with the question of how Socratic dialectic, as a search for Forms or essences, is possible.

Scepticism and Ontological Status

The plain man, on being told that holiness 'is something' or 'is a reality', or that he is to look to it as a standard for determining the propriety of his actions, may very well be expected to say, 'All right. Where is it?' And this request for a location, naïve enough in itself, disguises a genuine question: If holiness is real, what sort of reality has it got? If it exists, how does it exist?

These are questions of ontological status, but they are not to be answered by citing non-identity or priority, which are relations, for they are questions about the Forms which are supposed to stand in those relations. They are questions, to be precise, not about what any given Form is, but about what it is to be a Form. Mr Richard Robinson remarks:[1]

> The greatest single innovation of the middle dialogues is no doubt that Socrates, instead of inquiring after particular 'essences' or 'forms' as he previously did, now begins to talk about the whole body of 'forms', and is as much concerned about the nature of a 'form' in general as he is about any particular 'form'.

The middle dialogues ascend to a new level of generality: they ask what it is to be a Form, and answer the question with a doctrine of Two Worlds. In the *Euthyphro* and other early dialogues, that question, so far from being answered, is left unraised.

It is left unraised because the theory of Forms in the early dialogues, though a technical and metaphysical theory, is essentially continuous with common sense, and because, therefore, there is a naturalness about the 'What is it?' question which disguised its novelty. We all believe, for example, that there is such a thing as punctuality, and that punctuality is a virtue; and, believing this, we might easily be led by questioning to attempt to say what punctuality as such is. In Socratic hands, this will involve the use of a highly sophisticated existence assumption, the assumption that there is a Form of punctuality, and that it is a universal, standard, and essence; if this assumption is thought through far enough, punctuality will be seen to be prior to and not identical with instances of punctuality. Still, the whole inquiry will be directed toward determining *what* punctuality is, not *whether* it is. The progress of discussion will appear as a passage from vagueness and confusion toward clarity, not as a reflection on the furniture of the universe. And so long, therefore, as inquiry remains untroubled by sceptical doubts, the common-sense belief that there is such a thing as punctuality, even when common sense has been stretched by Socratic inquiry into a reflection on essence, will not suggest the question, 'Where is it?'[2]

[1] *PED*, p. 61.

[2] It will be observed that the question of existence and the question of ontological status are two questions, not one. The first question is prior to the second, in that it must be answered affirmatively before the second can be raised; to ask the ontological status of a thing agreed not to exist is to ask a nonsense question. Again, the first question is independent of the second, in that while the second does not arise if

The reason is that the 'Where is it?' question, when it demands an account of ontological status, is a mark of intellectual discontent. It is pointless to ask the location of punctuality – pointless, that is, until the uncriticized assumption that there is such a thing is called in question, and we are compelled to stop and render an account. Common sense will not demand that account: of course there is such a thing as punctuality – see all the punctual people. Nor will Socratic inquiry demand it: the aim of dialectic in the *Euthyphro* is not to prove that a Form of holiness exists, or that it can be defined. Those things are taken for granted. The aim is only to define it – to say what, not whether, it is.

An answer to the 'Where is it?' question, as distinct from the 'What is it?' question, will seem required only when the existence of Forms is doubted rather than assumed, only when the possibility of real definition, and with it the pursuit of dialectic, is challenged rather than taken for granted. This question was first forced on Plato's mind by a problem of *a priori* knowledge, broached in the *Meno* by the doctrine of Recollection.[1]

Scepticism and a Priori *Knowledge*

It is customary to rank the *Meno* as an early middle dialogue, and this is not unreasonable. Its prose style is indistinguishable from

---

[1] It is tempting to conjecture that the question was also forced on Plato's mind by Sophistry, and especially the moral scepticism involved in its claims. But this is not supported by the evidence of the dialogues. The *Euthydemus* presents a contrast between two sorts of protreptic toward virtue; that practised by Socrates, and that which Sophistry in its debased forms had tended towards; but the existence of virtue itself is never in doubt. Protagoras is portrayed as believing that there is

---

there is a negative answer to the first, an affirmative answer to the first is compatible with any consistent to the second. In short, it is possible to assume an answer to the question of whether Forms exist without assuming an answer to the question of how they exist, or what their ontological status is.

This point has sometimes been neglected. Professor Ryle, referring to the theory of Forms, has said that, 'A philosophical problem is, at the start, dominated by a status-question. Later this status-question surrenders its primacy, and even its interest, to a network of constitution-questions.' ('Plato's *Parmenides*,' *SPM*, p. 119.) But so far as the early dialogues are concerned – though not, surely, so far as the development of philosophy in this century is concerned – this puts matters backwards. Constitution-questions – questions of definitions, for example, and of the relations holding between terms such as holiness and justice, or virtue and teachability – are explicit and important in the early dialogues. Status questions are not.

that of the early period; but its concern for Recollection and the immortality of the soul, its use of a method of hypothesis borrowed from geometry, and its distinction between knowledge and opinion are early statements of themes which were later to occupy a large place in the *Phaedo* and *Republic*. Because this is so, it has often been thought that the *Meno* was written after Plato's return to Athens from his first journey to Italy and Sicily in 387 B.C.; while in Italy, he had been in intimate contact with Archytas of Tarentum, the leading Pythagorean mathematician and philosopher of his day. It is therefore plausible to conjecture that the *Meno* is a boundary-dialogue, which bespeaks the stimulus of new questions and ideas not yet assimilated into the completed synthesis of the *Phaedo*.

The *Meno* begins, as many early dialogues had begun, with a 'What is it?' question. Meno is asked to say what virtue is, not in order to distinguish instances of it, as in the *Euthyphro*, but in order to determine what properties are connected with it – specifically, whether it is teachable, or acquired by practice, or present by nature. As in earlier dialogues, Socrates quickly reduces his respondent to perplexity; but the discussion does not, as it would have earlier on, end there. For Meno, having failed to answer the 'What is it?' question, suggests that there may be no point in asking it. As Socrates sums up his argument (80e):

> It is impossible for a man to inquire either into what he knows or into what he does not know. He cannot inquire into what he knows, for he knows it, and there is no need for inquiry. He cannot inquire into what he does not know, for he does not know what it is he is to inquire into.

This paradox has some resemblance to the foolish paradoxes about learning introduced in the *Euthydemus*,[1] and Socrates labels it a piece of eristic (80e). But it would be a mistake to dismiss it as a

[1] See 275d–278c, 295e–296d.

---

such a thing as justice, though ignorant of what it is. Callicles rejects conventional justice as fit only for slaves, but puts a notion of natural justice in its place (*Gorgias* 484a–c). So too Thrasymachus (*Republic*, I, 338c). And Socrates himself would have supposed, no more than Callicles or Thrasymachus, that justice is to be identified with our conventional notions of it. He disagreed with the Sophists, not about whether justice exists, but what it is. And he supposed that dialectic, so far from being jeopardized by this issue, was a means of settling it.

sophism, for, in order to solve it, Socrates does not attempt to correct its logic, as he does in the *Euthydemus*, but rather introduces the doctrine of Recollection. Serious answers bespeak serious questions.

The reason why Socrates takes the paradox seriously is not far to seek. F. H. Bradley once remarked:[1]

> The want of an object, and, still more, the search for an object, imply in a certain sense the knowledge of that object. If a man supposed that he could never tell when possession is or is not gained, he surely never would pursue. In and by the pursuit he commits himself to the opposite assumption, and that assumption must rest on a possession which to some extent and in some sense is there. Naturally, I do not mean that at the start the philosopher has propositions which he lays down in advance. I mean that his action has no sense unless he does assume, or, if asked, would assume, that, when he has got propositions, he is able to judge of them, and can then tell whether they do or do not put him in ideal possession of reality.... Hence the only scepticism in philosophy which is rational must confine itself to the denial that truth so far and actually has been reached.

Meno's paradox has little enough to do with inquiry into the exact date of the Battle of Marathon, or the menu of yesterday's breakfast. But it has much to do with the sort of inquiry involved in Socratic dialectic. Consider the search for a definition of holiness in the *Euthyphro*. Does Euthyphro know what holiness is? Then the search is pointless, since if he knows he can say, and dialectic will have succeeded without beginning. Perhaps then Euthyphro is ignorant of what holiness is. But why then ask him to define it? Being ignorant, he will have no ground for deciding that one answer to the Socratic question is more appropriate than another, no criterion by which to tell when he has hit the right answer or offered a wrong one: dialectic, because it depends on the respondents' own efforts after truth, becomes mere fumbling in the dark, and the nerve of inquiry has been cut.[2]

---

[1] *Essays on Truth and Reality*, p. 16.

[2] Bluck (*Meno*, p. 8) argued that Socrates could have answered the paradox in a common-sense way by holding (i) that it is possible not to know what virtue is, and yet (ii) to know that it is what justice, courage, and so on, have in common, so as to (iii) use one's knowledge as a criterion for determining when one has discovered what virtue is.

The pressure of Meno's paradox is increased rather than relieved by Socrates' assumption that Forms are standards. One cannot gain knowledge of holiness by inspecting holy things, since one cannot determine what things are holy without knowledge of holiness. Euthyphro cannot, therefore, look to his everyday world for an answer to the 'What is it?' question. Nor is there any easy appeal to intellectual intuition available, since that implies inquiry, and the paradox requires an explanation of how inquiry is possible.

Socrates solves the paradox by slipping between its horns. The paradox assumes a dichotomy between explicit knowledge and absolute ignorance. Suppose, however, that learning and inquiry are recollection; if that is so, then to inquire is to bring what is already implicitly known to explicit awareness.

It is relevant to notice that this account is put forward, not as an ordinary part of dialectic, not as an attempt to say what virtue is, but as an attempt to explain how dialectic is possible – that is, to explain how the question 'What is virtue?' may reasonably be asked and answered. The paradox, by challenging this possibility, raises an obvious metaphysical issue. Dialectic aims at real definition; it assumes the existence of Forms. If dialectic, as a pattern of inquiry, is impossible, there is no good ground for supposing that the objects of its inquiry, since there is no knowledge of them, exist.

The justification given for Recollection is tentative enough. A slave ignorant of geometry is made to recollect the truth of a fairly difficult theorem with no aid other than the figures inscribed in the sand at his feet and the assistance of intelligent questioning. This shows the truth of Recollection. But Socrates has reservations in the matter: he is not certain that the doctrine of Recollection is true, but only that 'If we believe it our obligation to inquire into that of which we are ignorant, we shall be better men' (*Meno*, 86b). The reason for this reservation is not far to seek. There is in the *Meno* no clear account of how we come by our recollected knowledge, nor what the status of its objects may be. There is no answer, except at the level of popular mythology, to the 'Where is

---

But this does not solve the paradox. If one did not know what virtue is, then on Socratic principles one could not know that it is what courage and justice have in common. Cf. *Republic*, I, 354c.

it?' question as asked either of Forms or the pre-existing soul. Yet that question cannot be avoided if Recollection is true. The theory of Recollection in the *Meno* serves only the purpose of allowing dialectic to proceed. It is itself incomplete, a theory *ad hoc*.

Recollection and Deficiency

In the *Phaedo*, a different spirit is stirring, the spirit of a man who has thought things through and come to a conclusion. The discussion of Recollection there begins with a summary of the *Meno's* argument (*Phaedo*, 73a), but proceeds, as we have seen, to a new account based on the deficiency of sensibles with respect to Forms. The doctrine of Recollection, prompted in the *Meno* by need to justify Socratic dialectic, has become a means by which the gulf between Two Worlds is bridged.

This new ontology is a solution to sceptical doubts. It was almost certainly suggested to Plato's mind by geometry. Protagoras, probably in his lost work *On Mathematics*,[1] had argued that geometry is inapplicable to the physical world: there are analogues in nature, but no physical equivalents, to the geometer's breadthless lines and lengthless points.[2] Protagoras inferred from this, 'So much the worse for geometry'. Plato drew a different conclusion. Geometry is knowledge, clear and certain. If the physical world does not satisfy its requirements, so much the worse for the physical world. The geometer, working with straight-edge and compass, performs constructions in the sand. But though his tools are physical, and his language – Plato thought misleadingly[3] – the language of physical operations, the truth he gains is not a truth about physical objects; his constructions are rather images, inaccurate likenesses, of the things toward which his thought is directed.[4] Thus, for example, a geometrical line is tangent to a geometrical circle at one and only one point. But a physical line touches a physical circle, not at a point, but through a segment of straight line and arc. Curved line and straight coincide over a distance – a geometrical absurdity and a physical fact.[5] The

---

[1] See Diogenes Laertius, IX, 55.   [2] See *Ar. Meta.*, I, 997b, 35.
[3] *Republic*, VII, 527a–b; cf. *Phaedo*, 96e–97b.
[4] *Republic*, VI, 510d–e.
[5] See *Epistle*, VII, 343a–b.

theorems of geometry, then, hold only fitfully for the constructions in sand by which they are indirectly demonstrated. This is so, not because the geometer's instruments are too blunt or his operations too clumsy, but because the conditions under which his theorems hold are themselves geometrically rather than physically defined; physical objects, qualified as they are by geometrical predicates, fail to satisfy the conditions implied by those predicates. Sensible diagrams are likenesses of geometrical relations – they remind us of them. And they are good likenesses, since otherwise they would not be useful in discovering theorems or constructing proofs. But they are also deficient likenesses. Their deficiency is not one of degree, but of kind; physical figures are analogues which cannot in principle become equivalents of geometrical figures.

The relevance of this to the theory of Forms is direct. Plato in the *Phaedo* assumes that sensible instances of equality, which are also instances of inequality, therefore deficiently resemble equality, and that since this judgement rests on comparison, we must have had prior knowledge of equality in and of itself. The foundation on which this argument rests must have been suggested, at least in part, by an analogous deficiency of physical figures in geometry.

An analogy is not an equivalence. The relation of physical circles to geometrical circles is different from the relation of any sort of circles to circularity. But the truth remains that geometry, for Plato, illuminated metaphysics, and suggested a far-reaching answer to the problem of ontological status posed by Recollection.[1]

5. CONCLUSION

In the year 1663, shortly before Commencement, a thesis sheet was circulated in Harvard College. In those happy, long-gone days, a Harvard Commencement was an orgy of gluttony, punctuated by formal debates. The sheet provided topics. It offered for debate the proposition that *Ethica est vitiorum Emplastrum corrosivum*, which, roughly translated, means that the study

---

[1] For further discussion, see 'Participation and Prediction in Plato's Middle Dialogues', *SPM*, ch. iv.

of moral philosophy is a porous plaster for vice. As befitted a college whose curriculum still preserved the outlines of the medieval *trivium* and *quadrivium*, the science of Grammar was not forgotten either; students were asked to debate whether *Ha Ha He vox est hilaris bene Nota*, whether *Ha Ha He* is an expression well known to indicate mirth. But the mainstay of the *trivium*, after all, was Logic, and Logic was remembered in a thesis bearing on the ancient and honourable problem of universals: *Universalia sunt in se* ἀειφανεῖς *in re* ἀφανεῖς *Asterismi* – 'Universals are little stars, in themselves ever shining, but invisible in things.'

The thesis sheet, of course, was a spoof, circulated by a crew of Junior Sophisters bent on staging a mock Commencement. Even in that day, it seems, undergraduates combined a certain irreverence for academic propriety with the talent for ingenious waste of time. No doubt the whole thing was a source of concern to their faculty – all six of their faculty, it may be, with President Chauncy at their head.

In 1663 Junior Sophisters everywhere would have associated the light of those ever-shining and invisible little stars with the Music of the Spheres. They would have known, as Lorenzo knew before them and told Jessica, that 'there's not the smallest orb that thou behold'st but in his motion like an angel sings, still quiring to the young-eyed cherubins'. And they would have found it easy to suppose that, as with sound, just so with light. The light of the little stars is invisible, as the music of their motion is inaudible, because, 'whilst this muddy vesture of decay doth grossly close it in', we cannot see it.

A pretty thought. But the company at a mock Commencement is likely to prove frivolous, and it surely occurred to some downright soul to argue, at the expense of good poetry, that the light of those little stars was in fact a twinkle in the mind's eye of the beholder. Nominalists, like the poor, are always with us.

This scepticism suggests a certain division of question. There is the question of the stars, of course; it is one which philosophers and logicians still debate, or at least debate why they should not debate it. But then there are also various questions about the twinkle – about who has had it, and why he had it, and when. It is one such question that I have debated in this book.

I have argued – perhaps at this point it needs no repetition – that Plato's early dialogues, and specifically the *Euthyphro*, contain a theory of Forms, and further, that that theory is not to be identified with the theory of Forms found in the *Phaedo* and *Republic*. In the early dialogues, the theory of Forms is the foundation of Socratic dialectic, which assumes the existence of a distinct class of entities as objects of its search. In the middle dialogues, however, the theory of Forms is offered to provide an account of ontological status unlike anything the early dialogues can show; the questions it is meant to answer are not questions which arise *in* Socratic dialectic, but questions *about* Socratic dialectic – specifically, about its possibility, as a search for real definitions. These questions are first raised in the *Meno* by a paradox of inquiry and solved by the doctrine of Recollection; the practice of dialectic is then, and for the first time, seen to imply the possession of *a priori* knowledge. This claim, offered *ad hoc* in the *Meno*, is founded in the *Phaedo* and *Republic* on a new ontology of deficiency and degrees of reality.

The theory of Forms found in the middle dialogues, then, is neither the same theory found in the early dialogues, nor a different one. Not different, because it contains the earlier theory as a part. Not the same, because it is directed to issues the earlier dialogues do not raise. But if, in the *Euthyphro*, we do not find the full refulgence of a Platonic twinkle, we surely find a recognizable Platonic glint. And that, perhaps, is enough.

BIBLIOGRAPHY

ADAM, J., *Plato's* Euthyphro, Cambridge, 1890.
ACKRILL, J. L., *Aristotle's Categories and De Interpretatione,* Oxford, 1963.
ADKINS, A. W. H., *Merit and Responsibility,* Oxford, 1960.
ALLEN, R. E. (ed.), *Studies in Plato's* Metaphysics, London, 1965.
ARNIM, H. VON, *Stoicorum Veterum Fragmenta,* vol. iii, Berlin, 1923.
AUSTIN, J. L., *Philosophical Papers,* Oxford, 1961.
BLUCK, R. S., *Plato's* Meno, Cambridge, 1961.
BRADLEY, F. H., *Essays on Truth and Reality,* Oxford, 1914.
BURNET, J., *Early Greek Philosophy* (4th ed.) London, 1930.
—— *Greek Philosophy: Thales to Plato,* vol. i, London, 1948.
—— *Plato's* Euthyphro, Apology *and* Crito, Oxford, 1924.
CHERNISS, H. F., *Aristotle's Criticism of Plato and the Academy,* vol. i, Baltimore, 1944.
—— *The Riddle of the Early Academy,* Berkeley and Los Angeles, 1945.
COLLINGWOOD, R. G., *Philosophical Method,* Oxford, 1952.
CORNFORD, F. M., *From Religion to Philosophy,* London, 1912.
—— *Plato's Cosmology,* London, 1937.
—— *Plato and Parmenides,* London, 1939.
—— *Plato's Theory of Knowledge,* London, 1935.
—— *Thucydides Mythistoricus,* London, 1907.
DENNISTON, J. D., *The Greek Particles* (2nd ed.), Oxford, 1959.
—— *Greek Prose Style,* Oxford, 1952.
DIELS, H., and KRANZ, W., *Die Fragmente der Vorsokratiker* (8th ed.), Berlin, 1956.
DICKENSON, L., *The Greek View of Life,* New York, 1930.
DITTMAR, H., *Aischines von Sphettos,* Berlin, 1912.
DODDS, E. R., *Plato's* Gorgias, Oxford, 1959.
DÜRING, I., and OWEN, G. E. L. (eds.), *Aristotle and Plato in the Mid-Fourth Century,* Göteborg, 1960.
FIELD, G. C., *Plato and His Contemporaries,* London, 1948.
GAISER, K., *Platons Ungeschriebene Lehre,* Stuttgart, 1963.
GOODENOUGH, E., *Jewish Symbols in the Greco-Roman Period,* vol. iv, New York, 1954.
GOULD, J., *The Development of Plato's Ethics,* Cambridge, 1955.
GROTE, G., *Plato and Other Companions of Socrates,* London, 1865.

GRUBE, G. M. A., *Plato's Thought*, London, 1958.
GULLEY, N., *The Philosophy of Socrates*. London, 1968.
GUTHRIE, W. K. C., *The Greeks and Their Gods*, London, 1950.
—— *Plato: Protagoras and Meno*, London, 1956.
HARDIE, W. F. R., *A Study in Plato*, Oxford, 1936.
HAVELOCK, E. A., *Preface to Plato*, Cambridge, Mass., 1963.
HEATH, T. L., *History of Greek Mathematics*, Oxford, 1921.
—— *The Thirteen Books of Euclid's* Elements, New York, 1956.
HEIDEL, W. A., *Plato's* Euthyphro, New York, 1902.
HOUSMAN, A. E., *M. Manilli Astronomicon*, vol. i, Cambridge, 1937.
JOSEPH, H. W. B., *Introduction to Logic* (2nd ed.), Oxford, 1946.
KIRK, G. S., and RAVEN, J. E., *The Presocratic Philosophers*, Cambridge, 1957.
KNEALE, W., and KNEALE, M., *The Development of Logic*, Oxford, 1962.
KRAMER, H. J., *Arete bei Platon und Aristoteles*, Heidelberg, 1959.
MILL, J. S., *A System of Logic*, London, 1843.
MORROW, G., *Plato's Cretan City*, Princeton, 1960.
NILSSON, M. P., *A History of Greek Religion* (2nd ed.), Oxford, 1952.
OWENS, J., *The Doctrine of Being in the Aristotelian Metaphysics* (2nd ed.), Toronto, 1963.
RAVEN, J. E., *Plato's Thought in the Making*, Cambridge, 1965.
RICHARDS, I. A., *Why So, Socrates?*, Cambridge, 1964.
ROBINSON, R., *Plato's Earlier Dialectic* (2nd ed.), Oxford, 1948.
ROSS, W. D., *Aristotle's* Metaphysics, vol. i, Oxford, 1924.
—— *Plato's Theory of Ideas*, Oxford, 1951.
SCHANZ, M., *Euthyphron*, Leipzig, 1887.
STENZEL, J., *Plato's Method of Dialectic* (trans. D. J. Allan), Oxford, 1940.
—— *Zahl und Gestalt bei Platon und Aristoteles*, Berlin, 1933.
SMYTH, H. W., *Greek Grammar*, Cambridge, Mass., 1920.
TAYLOR, A. E., *Commentary on Plato's Timaeus*, Oxford, 1928.
—— *Plato*, (4th ed.), New York, 1950.
—— *Varia Socratica*, Oxford, 1911.
TREVELYAN, G. M., *An Autobiography*, London, 1949.
VINOGRADOFF, P., *Outlines of Historical Jurisprudence*, vol. ii, Oxford, 1922.
WEDBERG, A., *Plato's Philosophy of Mathematics*, Stockholm, 1955.
WITTGENSTEIN, L., *Philosophical Investigations* (trans. G. E. M. Anscombe), Oxford, 1953.

INDEX

International Library of Philosophy & Scientific Method

Editor: Ted Honderich

List of titles, page two

International Library of Psychology Philosophy & Scientific Method

Editor: C K Ogden

List of titles, page six

ROUTLEDGE AND KEGAN PAUL LTD
68 Carter Lane London EC4

International Library of Philosophy and Scientific Method

(*Demy 8vo*)

Allen, R. E. (Ed.)
Studies in Plato's Metaphysics
Contributors: J. L. Ackrill, R. E. Allen, R. S. Bluck, H. F. Cherniss, F. M. Cornford, R. C. Cross, P. T. Geach, R. Hackforth, W. F. Hicken, A. C. Lloyd, G. R. Morrow, G. E. L. Owen, G. Ryle, W. G. Runciman, G. Vlastos
464 pp. 1965. (2nd Impression 1967.) 70s.

Armstrong, D. M.
Perception and the Physical World
208 pp. 1961. (3rd Impression 1966.) 25s.

A Materialist Theory of the Mind
376 pp. 1967. (2nd Impression 1969.) 50s.

Bambrough, Renford (Ed.)
New Essays on Plato and Aristotle
Contributors: J. L. Ackrill, G. E. M. Anscombe, Renford Bambrough, R. M. Hare, D. M. MacKinnon, G. E. L. Owen, G. Ryle, G. Vlastos
184 pp. 1965. (2nd Impression 1967.) 28s.

Barry, Brian
Political Argument
382 pp. 1965. (3rd Impression 1968.) 50s.

Bird, Graham
Kant's Theory of Knowledge:
An Outline of One Central Argument in the *Critique of Pure Reason*
220 pp. 1962. (2nd Impression 1965.) 28s.

Brentano, Franz
The True and the Evident
Edited and narrated by Professor R. Chisholm
218 pp. 1965. 40s.

The Origin of Our Knowledge of Right and Wrong
Edited by Oskar Kraus. English edition edited by Roderick M. Chisholm. Translated by Roderick M. Chisholm and Elizabeth H. Schneewind
174 pp. 1969. 40s.

Broad, C. D.
Lectures on Physical Research
Incorporating the Perrott Lectures given in Cambridge University in 1959 and 1960
461 pp. 1962. (2nd Impression 1966.) 56s.

Crombie, I. M.
An Examination of Plato's Doctrine
1. Plato on Man and Society
408 pp. 1962. (3rd Impression 1969.) 42s.
II. Plato on Knowledge and Reality
583 pp. 1963. (2nd Impression 1967.) 63s.

International Library of Philosophy and Scientific Method
(*Demy 8vo*)

Day, John Patrick
Inductive Probability
352 pp. 1961. 40s.

Dretske, Fred I.
Seeing and Knowing
270 pp. 1969. 35s.

Ducasse, C. J.
Truth, Knowledge and Causation
263 pp. 1969. 50s.

Edel, Abraham
Method in Ethical Theory
379 pp. 1963. 32s.

Fann, K. T. (Ed.)
Symposium on J. L. Austin
Contributors: A. J. Ayer, Jonathan Bennett, Max Black, Stanley Cavell,
Walter Cerf, Roderick M. Chisholm, L. Jonathan Cohen, Roderick Firth, L. W.
Forguson, Mats Furberg, Stuart Hampshire, R. J. Hirst, C. G. New, P. H.
Nowell-Smith, David Pears, John Searle, Peter Strawson, Irving Thalberg,
J. O. Urmson, G. J. Warnock, Jon Wheatly, Alan White
512 pp. 1969.

Flew, Anthony
Hume's Philosophy of Belief
A Study of his First "Inquiry"
269 pp. 1961. (2nd Impression 1966.) 30s.

Fogelin, Robert J.
Evidence and Meaning
Studies in Analytical Philosophy
200 pp. 1967. 25s.

Gale, Richard
The Language of Time
256 pp. 1968. 40s.

Goldman, Lucien
The Hidden God
A Study of Tragic Vision in the *Pensées* of Pascal and the Tragedies of Racine.
Translated from the French by Philip Thody
424 pp. 1964. 70s.

Hamlyn, D. W.
Sensation and Perception
A History of the Philosophy of Perception
222 pp. 1961. (3rd Impression 1967.) 25s.

2*

International Library of Philosophy and Scientific Method
(*Demy 8vo*)

Smart, J. J. C.
Philosophy and Scientific Realism
168 pp. 1963. (3rd Impression 1967.) 25s.

Smythies, J. R. (Ed.)
Brain and Mind
Contributors: Lord Brain, John Beloff, C. J. Ducasse, Antony Flew, Hartwig
Kuhlenbeck, D. M. MacKay, H. H. Price, Anthony Quinton and J. R. Smythies
288 pp. 1965. 40s.

Science and E.S.P.
Contributors: Gilbert Murray, H. H. Price, Rosalind Heywood, Cyril Burt,
C. D. Broad, Francis Huxley and John Beloff
320 pp. about 40s.

Taylor, Charles
The Explanation of Behaviour
288 pp. 1964. (2nd Impression 1965.) 40s.

Williams, Bernard, and Montefiore, Alan
British Analytical Philosophy
352 pp. 1965. (2nd Impression 1967.) 45s.

Winch, Peter (Ed.)
Studies in the Philosophy of Wittgenstein
Contributors: Hidé Ishiguro, Rush Rhees, D. S. Shwayder, John W. Cook,
L. R. Reinhardt and Anthony Manser
224 pp. 1969.

Wittgenstein, Ludwig
Tractatus Logico-Philosophicus
The German text of the *Logisch-Philosophische Abhandlung* with a new
translation by D. F. Pears and B. F. McGuinness. Introduction by
Bertrand Russell
188 pp. 1961. (3rd Impression 1966.) 21s.

Wright, Georg Henrik Von
Norm and Action
A Logical Enquiry. The Gifford Lectures
232 pp. 1963. (2nd Impression 1964.) 32s.

The Varieties of Goodness
The Gifford Lectures
236 pp. 1963. (3rd Impression 1966.) 28s.

Zinkernagel, Peter
Conditions for Description
Translated from the Danish by Olaf Lindum
272 pp. 1962. 37s. 6d.

International Library of Psychology, Philosophy, and Scientific Method
(*Demy 8vo*)

PHILOSOPHY

Anton, John Peter
Aristotle's Theory of Contrariety
276 pp. 1957. 25s.

Black, Max
The Nature of Mathematics
A Critical Survey
242 pp. 1933. (5th Impression 1965.) 28s.

Bluck, R. S.
Plato's Phaedo
A Translation with Introduction, Notes and Appendices
226 pp. 1955. 21s.

Broad, C. D.
Five Types of Ethical Theory
322 pp. 1930. (9th Impression 1967.) 30s.

The Mind and Its Place in Nature
694 pp. 1925. (7th Impression 1962.) 70s. See also Lean, Martin

Buchler, Justus (Ed.)
The Philosophy of Peirce
Selected Writings
412 pp. 1940. (3rd Impression 1956.) 35s.

Burtt, E. A.
The Metaphysical Foundations of Modern Physical Science
A Historical and Critical Essay
364 pp. 2nd (revised) edition 1932. (5th Impression 1964.) 35s.

Carnap, Rudolf
The Logical Syntax of Language
Translated from the German by Amethe Smeaton
376 pp. 1937. (7th Impression 1967.) 40s.

Chwistek, Leon
The Limits of Science
Outline of Logic and of the Methodology of the Exact Sciences
With Introduction and Appendix by Helen Charlotte Brodie
414 pp. 2nd edition 1949. 32s.

Cornford, F. M.
Plato's Theory of Knowledge
The Theaetetus and Sophist of Plato
Translated with a running commentary
358 pp. 1935. (7th Impression 1967.) 28s.

International Library of Psychology, Philosophy, and Scientific Method
(*Demy 8vo*)

Cornford, F. M. (*continued*)
Plato's Cosmology
The Timaeus of Plato
Translated with a running commentary
402 pp. Frontispiece. 1937. (5th Impression 1966.) 45s.

Plato and Parmenides
Parmenides' *Way of Truth* and Plato's *Parmenides*
Translated with a running commentary
280 pp. 1939. (5th Impression 1964.) 32s.

Crawshay-Williams, Rupert
Methods and Criteria of Reasoning
An Inquiry into the Structure of Controversy
312 pp. 1957. 32s.

Fritz, Charles A.
Bertrand Russell's Construction of the External World
252 pp. 1952. 30s.

Hulme, T. E.
Speculations
Essays on Humanism and the Philosophy of Art
Edited by Herbert Read. Foreword and Frontispiece by Jacob Epstein
296 pp. 2nd edition 1936. (6th Impression 1965.) 40s.

Lazerowitz, Morris
The Structure of Metaphysics
With a Foreword by John Wisdom
262 pp. 1955. (2nd Impression 1963.) 30s.

Lodge, Rupert C.
Plato's Theory of Art
332 pp. 1953. 25s.

Mannheim, Karl
Ideology and Utopia
An Introduction to the Sociology of Knowledge
With a Preface by Louis Wirth. Translated from the German by Louis Wirth
and Edward Shils
360 pp. 1954. (2nd Impression 1966.) 30s.

Moore, G. E.
Philosophical Studies
360 pp. 1922. (6th Impression 1965.) 35s. See also Ramsey, F. P.

International Library of Psychology, Philosophy, and Scientific Method
(*Demy 8vo*)

Ogden, C. K., and Richards, I. A.
The Meaning of Meaning
A Study of the Influence of Language upon Thought and of the Science of Symbolism
With supplementary essays by B. Malinowski and F. G. Crookshank
394 pp. 10th Edition 1949. (6th Impression 1967.) 32s.
See also Bentham, J.

Peirce, Charles, *see* Buchler, J.

Ramsey, Frank Plumpton
The Foundations of Mathematics and other Logical Essays
Edited by R. B. Braithwaite. Preface by G. E. Moore
318 pp. 1931. (4th Impression 1965.) 35s.

Richards, I. A.
Principles of Literary Criticism
312 pp. 2nd Edition. 1926. (17th Impression 1966.) 30s.

Mencius on the Mind. Experiments in Multiple Definition
190 pp. 1932. (2nd Impression 1964.) 28s.

Russell, Bertrand, *see* Fritz, C. A.; Lange, F. A.; Wittgenstein, L.

Smart, Ninian
Reasons and Faiths
An Investigation of Religious Discourse, Christian and Non-Christian
230 pp. 1958. (2nd Impression 1965.) 28s.

Vaihinger, H.
The Philosophy of As If
A System of the Theoretical, Practical and Religious Fictions of Mankind
Translated by C. K. Ogden
428 pp. 2nd edition 1935. (4th Impression 1965.) 45s.

Wittgenstein, Ludwig
Tractatus Logico-Philosophicus
With an Introduction by Bertrand Russell, F.R.S., German text with an English translation en regard
216 pp. 1922. (9th Impression 1962.) 21s.
For the Pears-McGuinness translation—*see page 5*

Wright, Georg Henrik von
Logical Studies
214 pp. 1957. (2nd Impression 1967.) 28s.

International Library of Psychology, Philosophy, and Scientific Method
(*Demy 8vo*)

Zeller, Eduard
Outlines of the History of Greek Philosophy
Revised by Dr. Wilhelm Nestle. Translated from the German by L. R. Palmer
248 pp. 13th (revised) edition 1931. (5th Impression 1963.) 28s.

PSYCHOLOGY

Adler, Alfred
The Practice and Theory of Individual Psychology
Translated by P. Radin
368 pp. 2nd (revised) edition 1929. (8th Impression 1964.) 30s.

Eng, Helga
The Psychology of Children's Drawings
From the First Stroke to the Coloured Drawing
240 pp. 8 colour plates. 139 figures. 2nd edition 1954. (3rd Impression 1966.) 40s.

Koffka, Kurt
The Growth of the Mind
An Introduction to Child-Psychology
Translated from the German by Robert Morris Ogden
456 pp 16 figures. 2nd edition (revised) 1928. (6th Impression 1965.) 45s.

Principles of Gestalt Psychology
740 pp. 112 figures. 39 tables. 1935. (5th Impression 1962.) 60s.

Malinowski, Bronislaw
Crime and Custom in Savage Society
152 pp. 6 plates. 1926. (8th Impression 1966.) 21s.

Sex and Repression in Savage Society
290 pp. 1927. (4th Impression 1953.) 30s.
See also Ogden, C. K.

Murphy, Gardner
An Historical Introduction to Modern Psychology
488 pp. 5th edition (revised) 1949. (6th Impression 1967.) 40s.

Paget, R.
Human Speech
Some Observations, Experiments, and Conclusions as to the Nature, Origin, Purpose and Possible Improvement of Human Speech
374 pp. 5 plates. 1930. (2nd Impression 1963.) 42s.

Petermann, Bruno
The Gestalt Theory and the Problem of Configuration
Translated from the German by Meyer Fortes
364 pp. 20 figures. 1932. (2nd Impression 1950.) 25s.

International Library of Psychology, Philosophy, and Scientific Method
(*Demy 8vo*)

Piaget, Jean
The Language and Thought of the Child
Preface by E. Claparède. Translated from the French by Marjorie Gabain
220 pp. 3rd edition (revised and enlarged) 1959. (3rd Impression 1966.) 30s.

Judgment and Reasoning in the Child
Translated from the French by Marjorie Warden
276 pp. 1928. (5th Impression 1969.) 30s.

The Child's Conception of the World
Translated from the French by Joan and Andrew Tomlinson
408 pp. 1929. (4th Impression 1964.) 40s.

The Child's Conception of Physical Causality
Translated from the French by Marjorie Gabain
(3rd Impression 1965.) 30s.

The Moral Judgment of the Child
Translated from the French by Marjorie Gabain
438 pp. 1932. (4th Impression 1965.) 35s.

The Psychology of Intelligence
Translated from the French by Malcolm Piercy and D. E. Berlyne
198 pp. 1950. (4th Impression 1964.) 18s.

The Child's Conception of Number
Translated from the French by C. Gattegno and F. M. Hodgson
266 pp. 1952. (3rd Impression 1964.) 25s.

The Origin of Intelligence in the Child
Translated from the French by Margaret Cook
448 pp. 1953. (2nd Impression 1966.) 42s.

The Child's Conception of Geometry
In collaboration with Bärbel Inhelder and Alina Szeminska. Translated from the French by E. A. Lunzer
428 pp. 1960. (2nd Impression 1966.) 45s.

Piaget, Jean, and Inhelder, Bärbel
The Child's Conception of Space
Translated from the French by F. J. Langdon and J. L. Lunzer
512 pp. 29 figures. 1956. (3rd Impression 1967.) 42s.

Roback, A. A.
The Psychology of Character
With a Survey of Personality in General
786 pp. 3rd edition (revised and enlarged 1952.) 50s.

Smythies, J. R.
Analysis of Perception
With a Preface by Sir Russell Brain, Bt.
162 pp. 1956. 21s.

International Library of Psychology, Philosophy, and Scientific Method
(*Demy 8vo*)

van der Hoop, J. H.
Character and the Unconscious
A Critical Exposition of the Psychology of Freud and Jung
Translated from the German by Elizabeth Trevelyan
240 pp. 1923. (2nd Impression 1950.) 20s.

Woodger, J. H.
Biological Principles
508 pp. 1929. (Re-issued with a new Introduction 1966.) 60s.

PRINTED BY HEADLEY BROTHERS LTD 109 KINGSWAY LONDON WC2 AND ASHFORD KENT